GO WITH GOD

by

Norman (Norm) Achen, Attorney (Ret)

Lee Smart, Colonel (Ret)

SKETCH ARTIST

Roxanne Mather is an art student at University of California, San Diego, as is her identical twin. On Pages 113, 125 & 131 you will see her work.

Robert Bailey is a well-known airplane artist from Alberta, Canada. You will see my P-51 crashing into cows on page 55.

 **Trafford** PUBLISHING www.trafford.com

North America & international
toll-free: 1 888 232 4444 (USA & Canada)
phone: 250 383 6864 ♦ fax: 250 383 6804 ♦ email: info@trafford.com

The United Kingdom & Europe
phone: +44 (0)1865 722 113 ♦ local rate: 0845 230 9601
facsimile: +44 (0)1865 722 868 ♦ email: info.uk@trafford.com

10 9 8

DEDICATIONS

This book is dedicated to my mother, to Gail and Marilyn,
and to all the POWs, especially "Moose."

I found this letter to Saint Peter in a friend's scrapbook. It was dedicated
to those members of the 4th Fighter Group who gave their lives in WWII.
I suspect that, if I could find Ms. Elma Dean, she would not object to it
now being dedicated to all of our young combatants who have laid their
lives on the altar of freedom.

Norm Achen

Letter to Saint Peter
Let them in, Peter, they are very tired
Give them the couches where the angels sleep
Let them wake whole again to new dawns-fired
With sun. Not war. And may their peace be deep:
Remember where the broken bodies lie.
And give them things they like, let them make noise.
GOD KNOWS how young they were to have to die:
Give swing bands, NOT gold harps, to these our boys.
Let them love, Peter, they have had no time.
GIRLS—sweet as meadow wind with flowing hair.
They should have trees and bird songs, hills to climb.
The taste of summer in a ripened pear. Tell them
How they are missed. Say not to fear:
It's going to be all right with us down here.

Elma Dean

ACKNOWLEDGEMENTS

**Special thanks to the following people who
in many ways helped me write this book:**

Ray Toliver, Author of "The Interrogator"
and
Head of "Old Bold Pilots."

Robert Barney, Colonel (Ret), Author of "Bulletproof"
and a POW with me.

Scott Marchand, Director of Collection and Aircraft Restoration,
Pima Air & Space Museum, Tucson, Arizona.

Lee Smart, Colonel (Ret), my co-author who dedicated hours and
hours to help make "GO WITH GOD" readable.

Chris Scharff – A friendship that makes Divine Credence plausible
rather than pure luck.

TABLE OF CONTENTS

INTRODUCTIONS

"THE INTERROGATOR"

Raymond Toliver

In Chapter VIII you will meet Hanns Joachim Scharff who is immortalized by Ray Toliver in the book *The Interrogator*. In this book is a dedication by Hanns Scharff to the fighter pilots he interrogated. I quote: "This book is further dedicated to those stalwart, loyal, and brave unfortunates who are, or who have been, prisoners of war. Their unswerving faithfulness to principles and country have cost them happiness, health, and even their lives. These are the men and women who know the meaning of true character."

Many American fighter pilots have a story to tell about their experiences with meeting Hanns Scharff and I am one of them.

Sixty years later, I learned that the son of Hanns Scharff, Chris Scharff, lived within a mile of me in Carlsbad, California. We have become friends and often talk about his father and the war. He has provided the following:

"FOE OF MY FATHER"

by
HANNS CHRISTIAN SCHARFF

As the son of one of those extraordinary people who fought with dedication and so bitterly hard for their countries, I have had many a moment to reflect on them. They fought in the great conflict of WW

II and were of heritages that crossed the boundaries of the conflict, as did some of their spouses. My father, a German with a British wife, was one such person. One of his protagonists was of the same heritage as himself. Yet they had their duties and loyalties to the countries of their birth.

As soldiers they fought bitterly against one another and the irony of it all is that they mostly all respected each other during the years of the conflict, but were genuinely friendly with one another after the war. Another irony was that for not hating one another during the war, their respective countries' bureaucracies were sometimes too ready to charge their own countrymen with treason. Fortunately, often, saner heads prevailed.

My joy has been to meet onetime enemies of my father, Hanns Scharff, "The Interrogator", together with him and even now since his passing, with fighter pilots whom he interrogated. The wonder of it all is the respect they all had for each other's foes and the impression they appear to have made on one another.

It is a human tragedy that nations can get embroiled in the mayhem of war with all its attendant killing and misery and yet when it is all over, past enemies (can) become fast friends.

Hail and well met, Norman Achen, foe of my father.

Hanns Christian Scharff

THE LUFTWAFFE'S MASTER INTERROGATOR
This photo shows Hanns-Joachim Scharff just a few days after he was conscripted into military service.

7

DIARY OF JANUARY 1945 MARCH

Norm Achen

In this opening I have included one page of a diary I kept on this march. It was as close to a disaster as I ever want to come. Approximately 2,300 men started the march. I have never been able to find the exact figure. Close to 89 were unable to walk at all and were left in Sagan until boxcars were available to bring them to Nuremberg.

On the second night an additional 800 were not able to go any further. We were allowed to help some of those get into barns along the road. It was reported later that most had been rounded up and taken to Moosburg, Stalag Luft VII A.

r (EIGHT DAYS OF HELL)

JAN. 28, 1945

WE MARCHED THE NEXT 19 KILO IN ABOUT FOUR
HOURS. AT SEVEN IT WAS 10 BELOW 0. TRIED
TO STOP ONCE BUT IT WAS TO COLD. VERY BRIGHT
MOONLIGHT NIGHT. THE WHOLE REAR OF THE
COLUMN BROKE FOR THE WOODS ONCE WHEN
THEY THOUGHT THEY WERE BEING STRAFFED.
THE GOONS TOOK MANY SHOTS BUT ONLY HIT
TWO FELLOWS. ONE IN THE HEEL THE OTHER
IN THE HEAD. ALL HAD THERE BLANKETS
THROWN OVER THERE HEADS. IT LOOKED LIKE
AN ARMY OF GHOSTS. THE GUARDS WERE
NOW MUCH MORE TIRED THAN US. ONE GUARD
LET HIS PACK DROP FROM HIS SHOULDERS AND
DRAGGED IT BY THE STRAPS FOR AWHILE BUT
FINALLY LET IT GO ALL TOGETHER. ANOTHER
WALKING BESIDE US TOOK OF HIS AMMO. BELT
AND THREW THAT AND HIS GUN INTO THE WOODS
AND FELL IN THE COLUMN WITH US. WE FINALLY
STOPPED IN A SMALL CITY FOR AN HOUR BUT HAD
TO KEEP MOVING TO KEEP MOVING TO KEEP WARM.
ONE GUARD WALKED UP BESIDE ME, THREW
DOWN HIS PACK FELL ON IT AND SAID "THIS IS
THE END." QUITE A FEW MEN WERE LEFT HERE,
BUT WE MOVED ON. THE GOONS HAD GOTTEN A
HORSE AND WAGON HERE FOR THERE PACKS BUT
THE HORSE DIED LATER ON IN THE EVENING. IT WAS
NOTHING TO SEE ONE OF THE GUARDS CARRYING HIS
DOG IN HIS ARMS BECAUSE OF FROZEN FEET.

JAN. 29, 1945

WE ARRIVED AT MUSKOW ABOUT 0700. WE HAD
LEFT ABOUT 800 OUT OF THE ORIGINAL 2300 ALONG
THE ROAD IN BARNS. ALSO ABOUT 2/3 OF THE GUARDS.
THIS WAS DUE TO EXPOSURE AND FATIGUE. SITUATION
WAS REALLY QUITE BAD ABOUT THIS TIME. AND SO
WAS THE MORALE.

CONT.

9

EXTENSION OF REMARKS
OF
HON. GEORGE A. PADDOCK

OF ILLINOIS
IN THE HOUSE OF REPRESENTATIVES

Thursday, February 26, 1942

MR. PADDOCK: Mr. Speaker, as in every American war, our soldiers and sailors are displaying splendid courage, treating as daily duty exploits we call heroic, and among the news from the fighting front is an item I think it worthwhile to repeat.

Dispatches from the Bataan Peninsula report that Capt. Arthur W. Wermuth, Fifty-seventh Filipino Scouts, has with his rifle and submachine gun "absolutely accounted for" 116 Japanese in the course of actions which won him three decorations. On his first patrol, January 6, Captain Wermuth volunteered to locate an outpost pocketed by the Japanese advance; alone, he slipped through several thousand of the enemy, found his men, and brought them back.

A few days later he burned a village, single-handedly destroying the enemy encampment and escaping under artillery fire. He and 84 other volunteers cleaned out 300 snipers, killing 250 of them. The next week he took a few scouts and a visiting marine a mile and a half behind the Japanese lines on a reconnaissance, found a large bivouac, directed American batteries upon it, and returned with no casualties and a Japanese captain as prisoner. Twice he walked out of a hospital against orders 2 days after being wounded, not wholly healed but wholly ready for action. Captain Wermuth has been awarded the Silver Star for gallantry, the Distinguished Service Cross for extraordinary heroism, and the Purple Heart with two clasps for his three wounds.

It gives me particular satisfaction to make this brief mention of Captain Wermuth, since his residence of 3631 Janssen Avenue, Chicago, is the Tenth Illinois District, which I have the honor to represent. His father, who died a few years ago, was a surgeon well-known in Chicago; while his mother and sister are in Montreal, his grandparents and many relatives live in the Chicago area. His wife was a nurse at Ravenswood

Hospital when he met her, while studying under his father, the staff surgeon.

In these early days of the war when we face reverses with little good news to cheer us, it is a clear omen of final victory that men like Wermuth are proving again the bravery and the sound military ability of the American soldier and sailor. His valor, far beyond the normal call of duty, taking no heed of wounds or of the enemy's guns, positions, and superior numbers, reminds us what our men, given their chance, can and will do.

FEBRUARY 26, 1942

ARTHUR WERMUTH

May 1953: In Denver, Colorado, I met Arthur Wermuth and we became friends. The main reason was because we had been POWs, but on opposite sides of the world. For the next several years, when I would be in Denver, we often met for dinner to discuss our experiences. It gave me the first real chance to learn what a true hero was. Arthur was a prisoner of the Japanese from March of 1942 until September of 1945, when he returned to the United States in a hospital ship. Arthur died a few years ago, but I've got my money on him, that when I meet him again he will have already received the Heavenly Cross Award.

Norman Achen

This article by Colonel (Ret) Andre Debievre was published in the Official Newsletter of the P-51 Mustang Pilots Association – Spring 2003. Over 78,000 American Service Men and Women are still missing in action. Most are from WWII.

 ———————————————————————

Ceremony for a World War II Mustang Pilot

On the 22nd of February 2002, the wreckage of a fighter aircraft was found in a swampy field in La Longueville, France, a small town near the Belgian border. The aircraft was a P51 and the pilot was still in the cockpit with his wings on his flight jacket and his name on his name tag: Lieutenant William Wyatt Patton. The crash occurred on January 15, 1945 when flying a weather scouting mission in heavy fog.

The remains of Lieutenant Patton were sent back home to Missouri, USA, a few days later, after the military honors, and in France, on the crash location, an important remembrance ceremony was prepared for September the 29th. Just before this date, everybody remembers what happened to the World Trade Center. Everything was cancelled.

In fact, the ceremony was just delayed: French and US authorities decided it would take place on the 15th of January 2003, on the 58th anniversary of the crash. That's why so many people gathered together on that day in the church of La Longueville, linking together for the same prayers civilian and military personal. French, American people and others coming from England and Belgium. On the first raw stood Mrs. Connie Patton, the niece of the pilot, coming from Missouri.

After the religious service, people moved to the location of the monument erected to Lieutenant Patton's memory. Along the road, schoolboys and girls were waving small US and French flags. Several high rank representatives of both nations made speeches. Then, in the silence of this green countryside the bugle blared, followed by the national anthems.

A few miles from this place, in Feignies, is an old military fort used as a war museum. After being cleaned up, all the pieces of Lieutenant Patton's Mustang have been displayed in a special room of this fort. All people attending the morning ceremony were there in the afternoon to see Connie Patton, tears in her eyes, unveil the plaque of Lieutenant Patton's Memorial and discover what had been the shroud of her uncle for 56 years. As a former Mustang pilot, at the end of the ceremony, I handed over a plaque of the French air cadet association to the Mayor of Feignies. This plaque will be set in the Memorial.

Lieutenant Patton's mother and father never knew what happened to their son declared "missing in action", neither his two brothers and his sister. They all died wondering.

Colonel (Ret) Andre Debievre,
French Air Force.

PROLOGUE

When I first heard about Tom Brokaw's book, "The Greatest Generation", I wondered if I could qualify as being a part of this generation since most of his quotes were from his father and my father had died by 1930. I was unsure, but I bought his book and read it very carefully and thoughtfully. In fact, I read it twice.

I did not agree with Mr. Brokaw that ours was the "greatest generation," but I did feel we were different in many ways.

It was easy for me to feel this way. By the time we reached adulthood we had gone through three major changes. Most of the 1920s were the roaring 20s. Then came the Depression, and from there came WWII. Hitler thought Germany and Austria should conquer Europe, and then the world. Then the Japanese military bombed Pearl Harbor and we were in the war!

All of this thinking, and probably growing older, reminded me why I wanted to write a book.

· When I escaped from a German prison pamp and was reunited with my family in California, I was destined to meet and work for the Marx Bros. It was Harpo Marx who said, "Everyone should know what you veterans went through to preserve freedom for all of us. Please, some day, put it on paper."

I have finally done this, and I hope you approve of this effort. I would enjoy hearing from you if you like this book or even if you don't.

Norm Achen
P.O. Box 131793
Carlsbad, CA 92013

13

I

LEAVE WITHOUT PAY

My infatuation with airplanes was set in motion by an event that occurred when I was seven years old. My mother, two older brothers, and I had just moved to Casa Grande, Arizona - a seeming crossroad to nowhere in the middle of the Sonora Desert. We had been living in Wisconsin where my mother developed a breathing problem. Her doctor told her that she needed to be in a warm, dry climate for at least the winter. So my father drove us all out to Arizona where we ended up in Casa Grande in a house rented for the school year. My father returned to his business in Wisconsin.

We had barely settled in when the famous aviatrix, Amelia Earhart, flying what turned out to be the first solo cross-country flight by a woman, made an unscheduled landing on a desert road within a few hundred yards of our home. In the process of landing or taxiing, the cloth wings of her airplane sustained a number of small tears. My mother gave her a silk slip to cut up for patches. The next day her plane, all patched and fueled, was towed to a better road for takeoff. Amelia shook hands and thanked everyone and then she gave me a hug and took off. She circled once, buzzed the small, but admiring crowd (including me), and headed west away from the rising sun.

As young as I was, I knew that this was an extraordinary episode. Watching that lone woman climb into her airplane, and the magic of that plane sending up a cloud of dust as it roared down the road and lifted into the sky, had a profound and lasting effect on my young mind. Long after the aircraft disappeared, I stood there by myself, watching the endless horizon, imagining myself out there in the sky exploring the world.

The passion for flying was galvanized a few years later when, at the World's Fair, I got a chance to fly for the first time. My mother paid for

15

me to take a twenty minute ride in an open-cockpit airplane. We took off, circled to gain altitude, and flew out over Lake Michigan. I was a little frightened flying over the water, but exhilarated by the roar of the engine, the rush of cool air, the speed, and the complete feeling of freedom I felt up there. Then the pilot, over the intercom, told me to take the stick and steer the airplane. Telling me to push the stick slowly left and right, slowly up and down, he took me through the basic maneuvers. I was hooked. I wanted to be an aviator in the worst way.

In 1939, after completing prep school at Elgin Academy in Illinois, I returned to Arizona where I enrolled at the University of Arizona in Tucson. My general goal was to get a degree, but I hadn't yet developed any specific career aspirations. Since U. of A. was a land grant college, Reserve Officer Training Corps (ROTC) was required for the first two years. Those who wanted to continue enrolled in Upper Division and were commissioned as second lieutenants upon graduation.

In 1939, U. of A. ROTC had one of the last of the horse-mounted cavalry programs so a good bit of the training was spent on horseback. It didn't take me long to figure out that flying was a lot more comfortable than riding horses. At the end of my first year, it was announced that students could take flying lessons, get school credits, and a pilot's license if you passed the course. I jumped at the chance. As it turned out, flying over the desert in the heat of summer was not much different than riding a bucking bronco, especially if you're just learning to fly. But I stayed with it and qualified. My private license had four digits.

By April of 1942, the flags were waving, the bands playing "God Bless America," and on every wall was a life-size red, white and blue portrait of Uncle Sam pointing his bony finger at ME saying, "I WANT YOU." I wanted to finish college, but decided that my education would have to wait until I'd answered Uncle Sam's call. I knew what I wanted to do. I wanted to fly, and fly fast. Caught up in the patriotic fervor that was sweeping the country, I was ready to fight. In retrospect, I guess I understood the concept of war, but not the reality that "fighting" meant killing people, or being killed. I would learn the tragedies of that later, but for now, America was at war and I wanted to be a part of it.

There were openings for pilots in all of the services - Navy, Coast Guard, Marines, and Army. I had to make a choice. After careful consideration of all the factors, including how far I could swim, I volunteered for the Army Air Corps. I passed a battery of written tests and a rigorous physical exam, and was sworn in but told I wouldn't be called to active duty for at least four months. They called this waiting period "leave without pay."

The reason for the delay was simple logistics, or lack thereof. There were plenty of people like me who were ready to go fight. But although Uncle Sam was saying, "I WANT YOU," he was not yet ready to house, equip, train, or feed the hundreds of thousands of new recruits being inducted each month. In December of 1941, the Army Air Corps numbered 354,000. One year later, December 1942, the number had risen to 1,600,000, including me. Supply simply could not keep up with demand. So we waited.

Now the question was what to do until I was called to active duty? My mother and stepfather (my father died in 1930) were living in Phoenix so I decided to go there and see if I could find work for four months. Shortly after I arrived in Phoenix, I found out that they were hiring construction workers at the "Gila River Project." A contractor for the government was building a concentration camp for Japanese-Americans being rounded up, mostly on the west coast, and incarcerated. The construction site was in a remote desert area about twenty miles south of Casa Grande. I called the personnel office at the site and explained my circumstances to a man who identified himself as the hiring manager. I told him that I thought I could be a carpenter's apprentice. I don't know where I came up with that as I knew nothing about carpentry, but the man asked me a few discerning questions, such as did I know what a hammer, a saw, and a T-square were? When I answered in the affirmative, he declared me a carpenter and told me to come to work as soon as possible. I later found out that the carpenters union was just being nice to me because I was going into the service.

The government called these camps "Evacuation and Relocation Centers." At the time, I gave little thought to the significance of what they were all about. Two years later, in a prison camp in Germany, I fully understood. The Gila River Project was in fact a prisoner-of-war camp for citizens of the United States – Americans. It had the same appearance: wooden barracks, barbed wire, guard towers, and even the same crawl space under the barracks as the stalag I was in. Fifty years later, I drove out to the Gila River camp; one small building still stood, designated a "Memorial Center." I could not help but wonder, "What in the hell were we doing?"

I got a cot in the only hotel in Casa Grande, which cost me ten dollars a week. For an additional three dollars a day I got breakfast, dinner, and a box lunch. A movie was twenty-five cents; a pint of beer and a line of bowling, both a dime; and candy bars, three times the size of today's, a nickel. A bus took us to and from the site for a dollar. I don't remember just what my wages were, but with the limited choices for nightlife, I was able to save a whopping hundred dollars a week.

My first day on the job, I was instructed to make eighteen-inch square forms for cement. I applied my best saw and hammer work and by the end of the day, I had built about forty such forms. I examined my work carefully and was pleased. The forms looked squared to me. But my supervisor, apparently a perfectionist, saw it differently. So the next day I was assigned to the roof where I was to lay tarpaper. I'd watched a couple of guys working on the roof and thought that had to be pretty close to a job in hell. After a couple of hours on the roof, I knew I had underestimated... it couldn't possibly be that bad in hell.

In that part of Arizona in the summer, the temperatures would routinely go to one hundred fifteen degrees and higher. The thermometers topped out in the sun. The crepe soles on my shoes had almost completely melted off by noon. We would work about twenty minutes rolling out tarpaper and tacking it down. Then down the ladder to soak in and drink water, take two salt pills, and rest in the shade for ten minutes. Sunscreen was unknown, at least at the Gila River Project, and even though we wore huge hats, we still got sunburned. Exposed skin turned chocolate brown.

My situation significantly improved on the third day. I was moved inside and given the task of holding up drywall while a real carpenter nailed it in place. The message did not escape me, nor did it offend me... they didn't want me using a hammer.

After two weeks of holding drywall, an amusing turn of events occurred that would propel me into the fourth job of my short career. The project superintendent, "Ol' Supe," as we called him, was showing the lead man some details on a blueprint. After going over it two or three times, we heard him say, "You can't read blueprints, can you?" The lead man reddened a bit and admitted that he could not. Ol' Supe looked around at the several of us standing there and asked if any of us could read a blueprint. I waited for someone to speak up but when no one did, I stepped forward and said, "I can read blueprints, Supe."

Ol' Supe eyed me warily. Based on my somewhat spotty track record thus far, I'm sure he was skeptical, but he was in a predicament and desperate times call for desperate measures, so he beckoned me over to the print and tested me. When he realized that I could, in fact, read a blueprint, he grinned broadly, clapped his beefy arm around my shoulders, and said, "I knew we'd find your niche, Achen." I think he was elated to put me in a job where I couldn't do any more damage with my hammer and saw. I was made assistant to the lead man and given a twenty-cent an hour raise. Oh, happy me! I kept this job for the rest of my stay on the project.

In late September, I received word that I was to report for active duty in early November. I told Ol' Supe that I would be leaving on the following Friday. I tried to thank him for all he'd done for me, but he waved me off, saying, "Son, you and those like you are the ones to be thanked. Go with God." I have never forgotten those words or the feeling of pride that they gave me.

The following Friday, when I went to pick up my final check, I was surprised to find a crowd waiting to say goodbye. I was greeted with a cheer, cold beer, handshakes, and a "good luck and good hunting" send-off that I'll never forget. I tried to thank everyone and tell them how deeply moved I was, but for a "hero" going off to war, I was pretty choked up. I left with a good tan, my pockets full of money, and a great respect for the carpenters union.

Some sixty years later, while preparing notes to write about my wartime experiences, I began reminiscing about my days at the Gila River project. Though still greatly troubled by what we Americans did to fellow Americans at Gila River and other camps like it, I was grateful to the carpenters union for hiring me and treating me like I was special. After all, they didn't make policy - they simply made buildings. On a whim, I called the United Brotherhood of Carpenters in Phoenix to thank them. Of course, none of the present managers knew anything about the project, but the gentleman I talked to was polite and seemed interested. He asked questions about names, dates, the exact location, and any other details that I might recall. I answered as best I could remember and he thanked me for the call and for the information. A few weeks later I received this letter:

United Brotherhood of Carpenters and Joiners of America
Local Union No. 408

1401 North 29th Avenue
Phoenix, AZ 85009

TELEPHONE: (602) 484-0444
FAX: (602) 272-1977

December 24, 2003

Dear Mr. Achen:

The Carpenters Union supports our veterans and our Armed Services in every way possible. We are especially pleased that we were able to help you at the Arizona Gila River Project in 1942.

We thank you and all veterans for what you have done for the United States and we would like to present to you an **honorary lifetime membership** in the Carpenters Union. (Card enclosed).

We look forward to your book.

Sincerely,

William R. Martin
Senior Business Agent

Encl.

I suspect that Ol' Supe would have approved of the honorary membership under the condition that it did not qualify me to use a saw or hammer.

II

ACTIVE DUTY

November 21, 1942

I am here, Uncle Sam. I have finally answered your call and I'm ready to do what you ask of me. But please remember I want to fly! So put me in your finest and fastest, and I will make you, my family, and my country proud.

These lofty thoughts occupied my mind as my mother drove me to the base at Santa Ana on that most important day. As we approached the base though, I started thinking about how I was going to say goodbye to my mother. I guess I hadn't realized how close we had become over the years when often only she and I were there to take care of each other. Now, with one son, my older brother, already overseas, I knew it wasn't going to be easy for her; nor for me. "Goodbye and don't worry," didn't seem to make sense... of course she would worry. When the moment came, the best I could muster in a choked voice was, "Thanks for the ride and I'll see you at Christmas." I waved as she drove away and had to stay turned away from the military police at the gate for some minutes so that they could not see that this future hotshot fighter pilot was crying.

I was soon to learn that entering active duty was a process. You didn't go from being a civilian to becoming a soldier, sailor, etc., overnight. It involved a series of events: getting settled, assigned to a training unit, and specifically to a bunk in a designated barracks, meeting your peers and your drill sergeants, getting paid, and generally learning routines such as reveille, latrine and mess hall etiquette, bugle calls, K.P. duty, and lights out.

The training was also a process, or rather a series of processes. First was boot camp. This was, and is to this day, the basic training that every soldier goes through. Then came three phases of flight training: primary, basic, and advanced. Primary was a lot of classroom work and some flying. In basic flight, you really learned how to fly an airplane under many and varying conditions and circumstances; takeoff, flying and landing in good and bad weather, navigation, advanced maneuvering of the aircraft, and what to do in just about any conceivable emergency situation. Those who successfully completed primary and basic were then assigned to advanced training in fighter or bomber aircraft. About twenty percent went to fighters and the rest to bombers.

Boot camp, or basic training, in many respects was the toughest phase, at least for me. After wiping away the tears of farewell, I strolled into the base at Santa Ana with a smile on my face and hope in my heart. The smile vanished quickly when the M.P. started barking orders at me in what seemed to be an unfriendly manner. I was directed to a building where I was made to fill out a number of forms and questionnaires. I then reported to a captain who told me that this was my lucky day because I was going to be assigned to a squadron of Texans. It seems that a whole training squadron of Texans (240 men) had arrived at Santa Ana but one had fallen very ill, so lucky me was picked to replace him. The smile was gone and now hope began to follow. I spent several days early on fantasizing about how I was going to get even with the bastard who put me there.

The next several weeks were pure hell. The eyes of Texas were upon me and I withered under the glare. Two hundred thirty-nine Texans, most of whom had never been out of their county, let alone the state, versus me. I felt like I was in the Foreign Legion. In fact, I felt like I'd be far better off if I were. I know that things have changed a lot in the intervening years but in those days, Texans, at least the Texans in that squadron, only recognized Texans. All others were infidels. They treated me like I was a German spy. Things were going from bad to worse. I began considering mayhem, murder, and escape, in that order. Then something happened that changed all that.

One night, just before lights out, something, I don't remember what, set me off and I finally went over the edge. Clad only in my shorts, I jumped up on my bunk and, with my fists cocked and pumping, shouted, "O.K., you sons of bitches, one at a time!" The startled Texans - there were about thirty on the floor - all stared. Several started moving to flank me. About eight bunks down from me was a Texan named Johnnie Godbolt. He stood six-one or so, weighed in at about two-ten, and I'd been told was an All-American end at Texas A & M. He was soft-spoken and mainly a loner. I'd had no previous encounters with him. He slowly rolled off his bunk, also clad only in his shorts, and started moving towards me. I thought, "Oh my Lord, I've made a huge mistake here. My war might just be over."

Johnnie walked up, stepped to my left, turned, held out his hand with two fingers extended, and said in a measured tone, "NO, TWO AT A TIME." I nearly fainted, whether from fright or relief, I don't recall. There was dead silence and no movement as Johnnie said goodnight to me and strolled back to his bunk. Everyone was in bed and the room was still silent when the lights went out a few minutes later. As I lay in the dark, my heartbeat slowed some but my thoughts were confused. I guessed that I'd learned two things: all Texans weren't bad, and if you were going to get into it with a crowd, it would be wise to have Johnnie Godbolt on your side. The next day, as I walked past Johnnie, I said simply, "Thanks." His entire response was an almost imperceptible nod.

For the next week or so, the Texans more or less ignored me. Then one night as I lay reading in my bunk, several of them approached me. I thought, "Oh, oh, where's Johnnie," but they just hemmed and hawed a bit and asked politely if they could have a word with me. I said, "Of course."

I don't remember the details of the conversation, but they apologized for having treated me unkindly and said that they had voted to make me a citizen of Texas. With that, they presented me with a handmade certificate proclaiming me a citizen of "The Great State of Texas." Over the next several days I had two hundred thirty-nine "new friends" shake my hand, slap me on the back, and congratulate me. In those few days, all the bad feelings were erased. Sadly, the certificate was lost sometime during the war, BUT MY ESTEEM FOR THE TEXANS WAS NOT.

For the first six weeks of boot camp, all trainees are quarantined; that is, restricted to the barracks, the training areas, the mess hall, and the medical facility. Our training consisted of marching, learning that hay foot meant left foot and straw foot meant right foot, how to stand at attention and parade rest, how and whom to salute, how to make a bed, polish brass, and prepare for inspection. Our hair was cut short and our trousers and sleeves cut long. They gave us enough shots to sink a medium-class cruiser and then marched us around to make sure the "venom" was circulating properly through our systems. We were kept busy sixteen hours a day and if the drill sergeant thought we were getting

23

homesick or otherwise disaffected, we scrubbed the barracks floor with a toothbrush. I often wondered what all of this had to do with flying an airplane, but wasn't given much time to dwell on it.

When we were told that there would be no lifting of quarantine over Christmas, I thought it would be a tough day for all of us. Then when I checked the duty roster and saw that I'd drawn K.P. for December 25th, my spirits really sank. But, like so many things unforeseen, it turned out to be a blessing. What none of us had expected is that the Army would actually do something nice for us, but they did. The cadre had planned a special day for us. We had a great turkey dinner with all the trimmings and special entertainment. Everyone was treated with courtesy and good cheer. It made me feel particularly good to be part of the process. We all returned to the barracks with a smile, short lived as it may have been.

The main personal problem I had during boot camp (after I became a Texan) was with the latrine facilities. The barracks was a two-story wood building that housed thirty cadets on each floor. Each floor had a latrine with four toilets and four sinks with mirrors. When seated on the toilets, you sat facing the backs of the men standing at the sinks. Conversely, when standing at the sinks, you were looking in the mirrors at the men sitting on the toilets. There were no partitions and, to make matters worse, there was no system to circulate the foul odors that permeated the latrine and surrounding area at certain times of the day. Shaving, washing, and brushing teeth was bad enough - especially trying to breathe only through your mouth - but in the mirror you could see four guys sitting on the pots. I had grown up in an atmosphere where using the toilet was a very private affair, not to be shared with anyone. I couldn't avoid the morning hygiene at the sink, but using the toilet was another matter, or at least I thought it was. In order to have some privacy, I would hold off, sometimes with great discomfort, until late in the day, often after lights out.

This foolish routine finally caught up with me. My rear end started itching and burning and it got worse as time went by. Finally one morning I dressed, strapped on my gas mask (which you had to wear everywhere) and reported to sick call. After a two hour wait, the medic (I assumed he was a doctor) called me in, gave me a quick examination, and told me I had external hemorrhoids that would have to be removed. I asked him, "When?" and he said, "Now." I wasn't all that crazy about being cut on, but then I wasn't given an option.

I undressed, was placed on a table, and strapped into a harness similar to those used for delivering babies. I was given a shot of painkiller in the rear and for the next ten minutes or so I could hear the scissors clipping away. I didn't feel any pain, but I couldn't see what was going on and I kept thinking "I hope I don't end up a eunuch." When the doctor finished, he wanted me to see the good work he had done so he took a mirror and showed me. I don't remember just what I said to him, but I think it was something about his bedside manner, and perhaps his ancestry. With that, he told me to get dressed and return to my barracks.

The walk, or I should say, the shuffle back to the barracks took about an hour. Somewhere along the way, the painkiller wore off and I felt like I was plugged up with a warm cue ball. The Captain in charge of the squadron, a senior regular Army type, saw me waddle in and asked what had happened to me. When I explained, he asked if I had received any special orders from the doctor. When I told him I had not, he was surprised and called the clinic. He asked to speak to the doctor who had operated on me and was told that there was no doctor present, nor had there been a doctor there all morning. Shortly after that, I was told to report back to the clinic. I said I couldn't walk that far, so I was provided a sedan and a driver. When I arrived at the clinic, a real doctor examined me carefully, and commented that whoever had clipped me had done a good job. He gave me some APCs and some written instructions to take back to the Squadron Commander. Young and resilient, I healed quickly. I never heard any more about my phantom doctor, nor did I ask.

Another memorable clipping job at boot camp was the bi-weekly haircut, but the clippers were electric and the results, if less painful, were far more visible. To me a haircut had always been an enjoyable experience. I would sit in the chair and relax, maybe even doze a bit, get a head and shoulder massage and pick up some fishing tips, a little local gossip, and perhaps a slightly off-color story or two. On top of all this, I got a decent haircut with scissors! The process usually took twenty to thirty minutes. At Santa Ana, a haircut, if the "barber" wasn't very busy, took about three minutes and included putting the cloth over you and spraying a strong smelling lotion on as he laid the electric shears down. A recipient of this lotion was easy to identify for several hours after a haircut, and on Fridays, when most of us got haircuts in anticipation of weekend pass, the entire camp smelled like a cheap bordello, or so I was told. The only consolation was that we all got the same treatment and the same result. So, depending on the eyes or attitude of the beholder,

25

we all looked bad or we all looked good. I basically tried not to look at myself.

The Sunday review came to be an event we all looked forward to. After the fourth or fifth week, when we'd all learned to march fairly well, we were allowed to take part in the 1600 hours parade (we'd learned by then that 1600 meant 4 p.m.) There were some forty squadrons marching at the military pace of one hundred twenty beats per minute to the music of a magnificent military marching band. As each unit approached the reviewing stand, the order, "EYES RIGHT," was sounded, and the American flag and the squadron guidons were thrust forward. All heads and eyes swiveled right as hands went smartly to the brow in salute to the reviewing officer, a Colonel, or sometimes a General, who just as proudly returned the salute to the future warriors passing by. It was a proud moment for all of us.

By mid-March of 1943, our basic training phase was winding down but, from what we could gather from the news, the war was not. Japan was beginning to feel the might of our carrier-based attacks, but still occupied most of Southeast Asia and the Pacific Islands from Indonesia to the Solomons. Hitler's armies were very much in control of the European continent. It had been four months since I had walked tentatively through those huge gates at Santa Ana Air base into the harsh reality of boot camp. I must admit that since Johnnie Godbolt had saved my bacon and I became a "Texan," life had been much easier for me. I felt like I had learned a lot, not only about soldiering, but also about self-discipline and coping in unfamiliar and sometimes tough situations. Some of these newfound strengths would serve me well in the months to come.

Now we were all ready and eager to move on. We had been trained, evaluated, and had each received what seemed like several dozen shots. Some wise guy conceived the phrase, "We must be soldiers now 'cause we've been inducted, indoctrinated, and inoculated." In our mixed feelings of boredom and anxiety it became a rallying cry.

But the big question for all of us was what now? Pilot training? Bombardier or Navigator training? Those few days while we awaited orders saw a marked change in the attitude of the student body. The big talk, loud laughter, and general grab-ass were gone... replaced by quiet conversation and serious preparation to move out. Duffel bags were packed, unpacked, and repacked. I guessed that most, like me, were desperately hoping to be selected for pilot training. But no one was talking much about it, I believed out of fear that they wouldn't get it and would be considered a failure in the eyes of their comrades. The hours went by slowly.

Woh! Woh! The orders were finally posted on the bulletin board, and Achen, right after Abbington, was going to Ryan Field in Tucson, Arizona. Pilot training! I knew nothing about Ryan Field but plenty about Tucson, since I had attended University of Arizona and had lived there with my family for several years. I had twelve days of leave before my reporting date at Ryan Field. I decided to spend the time with my mother and stepfather in Los Angeles.

As I left Santa Ana Air Base, I went through a range of emotions. I was proud that I had made it through boot camp, and even more so that I had done well enough to be selected for flight training. I revisited the weeks of hell I had gone through with the Texans, to the point where I really wanted to give Texas back to the Mexicans, and how everything changed the night Johnnie Godbolt stood by my side and said, "NO, TWO AT A TIME." As I rode into Los Angeles to my mother's place, I felt that I had learned a lot and that I was mentally and physically prepared for flight training.

When I arrived at my mother's house I was proud to see the two gold stars displayed prominently in the front window. I hoped that neither of them would turn black. My mother took me shopping with her several times; I suspected to show me off. She introduced me to most everyone we met and they all had kind and encouraging words for both of us. When she took me to her grocery store, the manager wouldn't even accept her ration coupons.

About the fourth day home I went to visit my older brother, Bob, at the Douglas Aircraft plant. Two summers prior I had worked at the Douglas plant during the week and as a doorman at the Bruin Theatre in Westwood on the weekends. Security was tight at the plant but, since I was in uniform and told the guard that I was there to visit my brother, they not only gave me a pass but also provided a guide to take me to where my brother was working. The guide then took my brother and me on a tour of the facility. I was overwhelmed by what I saw. The plant was in production twenty-four hours a day, seven days a week. The production lines, which seemed to be operated mostly by women, were turning out aircraft at a staggering rate. I hadn't remembered any women on the lines when I'd worked there. Seeing all these women turning out war-fighting equipment, knowing that most of their men were somewhere using the equipment to fight the enemy, made me think about the Japanese Admiral who right after Pearl Harbor had remarked that he was fearful that Japan had awakened a sleeping giant. I had no doubt that he was right.

Though I had been looking forward to and enjoyed spending time with my family and relaxing after the rigors of boot camp, I soon became restless and anxious to get on to Ryan Field and flight training. So when it came time to leave for Ryan Field, I was ready.

On the train trip to Tucson, I found out that civilian passenger trains had a very low priority. I believed we spent more time on sidings than moving forward, but the passengers were friendly and I heard few complaints. When I got off at Tucson, many said, "Goodbye" and "God bless you and all of our fighting men."

III

RYAN, MARANA AND LUKE FIELDS

Ryan Field has never been described as a luxury resort. Isolated in the desert thirty miles south of Tucson, Arizona, it was hastily constructed after the war began to train aviators in the first skill they needed to learn - how to fly an airplane. It was not situated or constructed for the convenience and comfort of the cadets. We used to joke that it was located in the middle of the desert to protect the general population from the miscues of inept would-be pilots. We may have been close to the truth, though I don't recall any serious accidents during my time at Ryan.

The primary flight trainer was the PT-22, built by Ryan Aircraft, for which the training facility was named. It was a single-engine, low-wing aircraft with tandem open cockpits. Compared to what I had previously flown, it had a powerful engine (about 90 horsepower) and a sleek look about it. When I first laid eyes on the PT-22, I pictured myself with leather helmet, goggles, and silk scarf trailing in the wind, looking a lot like Eddie Rickenbacker.

Our class was only the third class to be trained at Ryan Field. When we arrived, our Commandant of Aviation Cadets, Lieutenant Roman Wojelehowski, who for obvious reasons soon became Lt. Woji and later just Woji to the cadets, greeted us.

Primary flight training, simply stated, is the basics of learning how to fly. It consists of ground training (theory of flight) and flight training (practical application). Both phases are done simultaneously. Generally, because of the difficulty involved in flying over the desert in the heat of the day, flight training was conducted in the morning and ground training in the afternoon. In the nine weeks there we would spend about forty hours in solo flight and conduct some two hundred takeoffs and landings. Additionally, we did the other things that all soldiers do in training: stand formations, do calisthenics, march, stand inspection, clean our latrines, K.P., guard duty, and so on.

Generally speaking, my recollections of life at Ryan Field were pleasant. As a young man who had spent most of my formative years learning how to make do on my own, the lessons of communicating and interacting with others were probably as important to me as the flight training. I got along well with my peers and developed many lasting friendships. With my prior experience, I was able to help other cadets and many came to me for advice and encouragement. I enjoyed and took seriously the status of unofficial "Senior Cadet Aviator." Life was good.

Part of interacting and, next to flying, the most fun was the daily football game. It turned out that Lt. Woji had been an All-American fullback from some mid-western university so, in addition to performing his regular duties, he organized a daily late-afternoon "touch" football game. Unfortunately, there was no turf at Ryan Field, so we played on sand. There were several other ex-college players among the cadets, so the games were taken very seriously and the desire to win ran high. The "touch" - two hands below the belt - often turned into crunching tackles. As a ball carrier, I ended up on the ground more often than not. But if carrying the ball was risky, leading interference, or trying to tackle the ball carrier, was even worse. The blocking could only be described as vicious. I soon learned that once a week was enough for me. It took that long to even partially recover from the bruises and sand burns. Two events that occurred in our third week of training had a profound effect on me. The first event was a tragedy.

One part of our conditioning was an every-other-day run around the airfield. The distance was a little over three miles and the running surface was desert which meant ups and downs, deep sand, hard rocky areas, cactus and brush that had to be negotiated, and, even though we ran in the morning, the temperature was generally in the mid-eighties. This was not a jog. We were expected to complete the run in less than twenty minutes. It was a tough standard even for young men in fairly good shape from boot camp and it turned out in one case to be a recipe for disaster.

My good friend, Johnnie Godbolt, seemingly in superb physical shape and always somewhere in the front of the runners, dropped one morning in mid-run and went into a coma. Two hours later he was pronounced dead. I had skipped the morning classes and gone to the

30

hospital and waited, expecting to see his smiling face when they let me in to see him. When the attending doctor came out of the emergency room, he went over and spoke quietly to Lt. Woji and, though I couldn't hear what was being said, I knew that the news was dreadful. When the doctor walked away, Lt. Woji came over to me and, knowing that we had been close friends, put his hand on my shoulder and said barely audibly, "He's gone."

Gone! I couldn't believe it. I'd just talked and laughed with him that morning. I felt sick, like I had been kicked in the groin by a horse. I made my way through the rest of the day in a semi-trance. I skipped dinner that evening and walked slowly around the perimeter of the airfield. When I reached the spot where I guessed that Johnnie had fallen, I sat in the sand and reflected over the good times we'd had and what a really good friend and good person he'd been. After some time, I looked skyward and with some bitterness asked, "Why?" I really didn't expect an answer and never got one. But deep down I knew that I would meet up with Johnnie again, and when I did I would again thank him and in return he would give me that <u>very slight nod</u> that said so much.

Two days after Johnnie died, I was standing on the flight line waiting my turn to fly when a messenger told me I was to report to the Commandant's office. I thought, "Now what the hell have I done?" Everyone I knew who had been summoned to the headquarters had either had their butt chewed for some significant transgression or been counseled on their poor performance in training. I had received good marks on all my training efforts, and I couldn't think of any rules that I had broken, at least none that might have come to light. I was puzzled and not a little apprehensive. When I entered the Commandant's office, I was told by the orderly to be seated. Shortly, the intercom buzzed and the orderly said that Lt. Wojelehowski would see me now – oh, oh, the man himself!

I entered, stood ramrod straight, and gave the Commandant my best salute. He returned my salute and without asking me to sit said, "Achen, you have just been promoted to Flight Lieutenant of Flight A. This promotion is being posted on the bulletin board and will be announced at assembly later today."

With that, he got up, came around the desk, handed me my orders, and said, "Congratulations." I must have been standing there looking bewildered, because Lt. Woji said, "That's all, Cadet Achen, and you can go now." I saluted, managed an about-face, and left. As soon as I

31

got outside I stopped and read the order. It said in part, "and all Cadets coming under his command are strictly charged and required to be obedient to his orders as such." I thought of the twenty or so Texans in Flight A and wondered if they would willingly take orders from a newly anointed Texan, especially since Johnnie wasn't here to provide backup. They could cause me all kinds of trouble and I didn't need that – all I wanted to do was fly.

I returned to the flight line and did my hour in the air. After that there was dinner and then more classes. Nothing was said to me about my new status, so I figured that either the order hadn't been posted yet or no one had recently read the bulletin board. As I lay in my bunk after lights out, I pondered my situation. My thoughts were pessimistic. Then, as I was considering all of the risks and disadvantages of this assignment, it suddenly occurred to me that I was evading the real issue. I was afraid. Afraid that I was not up to the task for which I'd been chosen. Afraid that I would fail. The Texans and all the other negatives were just excuses. Once I faced this, I gained strength. I had been on active duty for about six months now and it seemed that every day there had been a new and different challenge. I had learned from every one of them. I knew I could do this.

The first reaction to my elevated eminence came at formation the next morning. Just before the squadron was called to attention, several cadets greeted me with, "Good morning, Commander." One asked, "Did you sleep well, Commander?" to which I smiled broadly and replied, "You bet!" And that's the way it went. My rapport with my peers had been good and they accepted the fact that I had certain responsibilities and reacted appropriately. Surprisingly, the Texans gave me no trouble at all and, in fact, set the example in being supportive. I again thanked Johnnie Godbolt for this and often went about the day unconsciously humming strains from the "Yellow Rose of Texas."

Fortunately, my command position did not change the personal friendships I'd established with many of my classmates. On weekend passes, which ran most often from Saturday to Sunday afternoon, the busses would take us into town. Over time a group of us formed that would head for the Congress Hotel where a private room adjacent to the main bar had been set aside for us. There we would while away the afternoon and evening, drinking beer, and recounting "war stories" from the training week and speculating on the future. We generally started the process with "Cardinal Puff," a drinking game that mellowed us out pretty quickly.

Sometimes on the weekends, I would take a couple of friends with me to the Mansur home in the Catalina Foothills. Mort and Pete Mansur were close friends of mine who were both away in the service. Mrs. Mansur, their mother, enjoyed having service people visit and had given me a standing invitation. Her lovely home was large, staffed with servants, and my friends and I were always made to feel very welcome. I was able to repay Mrs. Mansur's hospitality in one small way. Sugar was one of the commodities that was in short supply in those days, so I asked the lady who ran the cadet mess hall if I could store up the sugar that I would normally use at mealtimes and take it to my friend. After a short hesitation, she said, "Okay, as long as you don't mention it around." So I was often able to take a pound or so with me when I went to visit. Occasionally I would accompany the Mansurs' cook to the meat market and somehow the butcher was always able to find a little something extra in the cooler for us. I sensed that this was a reflection of how servicemen were being treated across America.

When we would leave on Sunday, Mrs. Mansur would always ask, "What time will I see you next weekend?" I would reply, "If I'm not in the brig, I'll see you around 1800 on Saturday." When I graduated from training at Luke Field in Phoenix some months later, I invited Mrs. Mansur and my mother to the ceremony. When both attended, I was one proud and happy Second Lieutenant!

By late May, we had completed our primary training and moved on to Marana Field, thirty miles west of Tucson, for basic flight training. Basic flight training is a step up from primary. The trainer aircraft, the BT-13, had a more powerful engine which allowed us to get into more intricate and advanced maneuvers. The biggest challenge at Marana was the summer heat. By noon, the temperature was usually 110 to 115 degrees and, Marana being the Cotton Belt of Arizona, there were thousands of acres of irrigation in the area. Dry desert heat is one thing, humid desert heat quite another. During the day airplanes on the ground became so hot you couldn't touch the outer surface with bare hands. We had to climb to ten thousand feet before it was cool enough to close the canopy. Flight training started at first light and stopped at noon. We did our calisthenics in the dark of morning before flight training and exercised at the swimming pools from four to six p.m. Ground training was conducted in the early afternoon and in the evenings in classrooms marginally cooled by swamp coolers. It was difficult to concentrate on the lectures. Swamp coolers also cooled the barracks, but they barely brought the temperatures below ninety degrees. At night, I would wet my sheets and put one down and the other over me. I had to get up at least once during the night and wet the sheets again.

In spite of the heat, the training went well and I was doing fine until I injured myself one day while negotiating the obstacle course. One of the Chinese cadets had challenged me to a race and, always eager to compete, I accepted. Going over one of the hurdles, my foot caught in a sand pocket and I went down. My ankle swelled so rapidly that they had to cut my boot off. It turned out to be a bad sprain. I was allowed to continue with my class but, since I could barely walk, was exempt from physical training. I hobbled to classes and the mess hall and when I was scheduled to fly they would give me a shot of Novocain and send me off. In about three weeks, I was fairly mobile again, but stayed exempt from P.T.

One of the more interesting aspects of Marana was training with the Chinese cadets who joined us there. In our indoctrination, we were briefed on the background of this development.

In 1937, Japan had invaded China and quickly routed the tattered, poorly trained and ill-equipped Chinese Army. Chiang Kai-shek, the leader of the Nationalists, pleaded to the U.S. for help. The U.S., as well as the rest of the world, ignored his pleas. A retired U.S. Army Air Force Major named Claire Lee Chennault was enlisted by Madame Chiang to go to China and take charge of the fledgling Nationalist Air Force. For the next four years, Chennault struggled to build a viable force that could at least slow the Japanese juggernaut. He succeeded beyond expectations considering what he had to work with. Then, in mid-1941, the U.S. Government abruptly changed policy, provided China with one hundred P-40 aircraft, and lifted the restriction on American pilots joining the Chinese Air Force. Thus, Chennault created what was to become the most renowned fighter group in aviation history, the "Flying Tigers."

By late 1942, we had provided China, which was now our ally in the war against Japan, with more aircraft. We had also developed enough facilities that we could train Chinese pilots in the U.S.

The Chinese cadets were excellent students, eager, intelligent, and very competitive. The only problem was they didn't speak English, so their instructions from the tower were in Chinese. In some ways this was good training for us because we learned to be very watchful at all times – like we were in a perpetual dogfight. It was particularly critical at the end of the flying day when as many as a hundred aircraft were trying to land at the main field. Landing instructions would come over the intercom in both Chinese and English and you could only hope that the controllers were getting it right. Amazingly, there were no major accidents, so I guess they were.

As the training at Marana drew to a close, the mood of the cadets became somber and, as had happened at Ryan Field, chatter and horseplay in the mess halls and barracks dropped off sharply. Everyone awaited the posting of orders to see if their next phase would be fighters, bombers, or some other crew training. Two days before we were scheduled to graduate, it was announced at morning formation that we were to go by the Squadron headquarters after 10 a.m. and pick up orders. At 10:01 a.m., I, along with most of the other cadets, was at the headquarters building to learn my fate. When I was finally able to fight my way through the crowd and get my envelope, I tore it open very carefully. It read, "Luke Field," with a reporting date two days hence. Luke Field, Phoenix, Arizona, Advanced Fighter Pilot Training. I was going to be a fighter pilot! Advanced fighter pilot training is the last step in preparation for being commissioned as an officer and assigned to combat aircraft. If you passed this phase, you were assigned to a single engine fighter, the P-39, the P-47, or our newest, the P-51 Mustang.

Advanced training, like primary and basic flight, was a nine-week course and, like the other phases, it consisted of a combination of ground and flight training. Much of the ground training was done in the Link Trainer, a simulator that was a mock-up of a cockpit in which the student learned instrument techniques and was subjected to various situations to which he had to react. There were also classes most days relating to what we would be doing in flight later on. Finally, there was a lot of individual weapons training. We spent so much time on the ranges - rifle, pistol, and even skeet - that the standing joke was that we were secretly being trained to become infantrymen.

We endured the ground training, but we all looked forward to the hours we could spend in flight. The training aircraft was the AT-6, a two-seat aircraft equipped for instrument training and aerial gunnery, with enough power to allow for advanced maneuvers and emergency procedures. We trained from 7 a.m. to 7 p.m., Monday thru Friday, and from 7 a.m. until noon on Saturday. On Sunday, we had a much-needed day of rest.

The first high point of this phase of training came in the third week when we were moved to Ajo, a training area near Phoenix, for two weeks of aerial gunnery. Most of the time was spent on air-to-air gunnery firing at towed targets where we learned to lead moving aircraft from varying ranges. The rest of the time was air-to-ground training – strafing – where we fired at stationary and moving targets from various angles and altitudes.

The second high point of advanced training came in the fifth week when we moved up from the AT-6 to the P-40. In every aircraft we had flown up to that point there had been a seat and controls for an instructor. The P-40 only had one seat and, although we had done a lot of solo flying, we would now by design be on our own. To emphasize this, the Chief of Training Branch told us, "You will be flying the P-40 for the rest of your training here. It is all yours. Treat it with the kindness and respect that it deserves, and it will treat you the same."

When the schedule came out that morning, I saw that I was scheduled for my first P-40 flight at seven the next morning. After my afternoon classes I went down to the flight line where the P-40s were parked and asked the crew chiefs if I could sit in the cockpit of one. Knowing that I was an eager student, excited at getting my first shot, they smiled and said, "Sure." All of us had been checked out at least twice in the P-40 cockpit but I wanted to do it one more time. I studied the instrument panel and went through the takeoff and landing procedures several times. When I was comfortable that I had it down, I sat with the canopy open and, looking at the spectacular starry Arizona sky, thought of Amelia Earhart and my first encounter with airplanes. I remembered standing there, a seven-year-old boy, watching her plane disappear and thinking that someday I wanted to fly. That was only fifteen years ago and the changes in aviation were astounding. Amelia Earhart was flying what was considered a state of the art airplane that had cloth wings, very scant instrumentation, and an engine that was maybe forty or fifty horsepower – and she was flying solo across the United States. Tomorrow I would be flying solo also, but not across the country, and in an aircraft with sophisticated navigational instruments, and an engine that cranked some twelve hundred horsepower. Amelia Earhart was assumed dead, but some rumors had it that she was marooned on an island somewhere in the Pacific and others that she was a prisoner of the Japanese. Wherever she was, dead or alive, the memory of her courage and tenacity was still an inspiration to me. I went back to the barracks and, as excited as I was, slept like a baby.

The next morning I was too excited to even consider breakfast so I ended up on the flight line at 6:30. By 6:50 a.m., I was parachuted up, strapped in, finished my preflight, and had my engine warmed and ready to go. I called the tower and requested instructions. On order from the tower, I taxied to a westbound runway and waited for instructions to take off. After what seemed like a long wait, but was probably only a few minutes, the tower instructions came. "P-40 forty-four, you are free to take off." When I pushed the throttle forward that morning and felt the power of the huge engine as the airplane leaped forward and shot down the runway, I experienced an exhilaration that gave me goose bumps all over and still does to this day when I think about it. I could hardly take my eyes off those eight feet of engine in front of me. About three-quarters down the runway, I reached rotation speed and, as I lifted off, I shook myself and said, "Okay, Achen, this is it. You're flying a real combat airplane. Treat it with respect."

I climbed rapidly to eight thousand feet, did a slow roll each way, a series of snaps right and left, and then a loop, followed by another loop that fell off into a controlled spin. I was awed by the power and maneuverability of the aircraft. When, after what only seemed like ten or fifteen minutes, I received instructions from the tower to come home, I was surprised. I looked at my watch and realized I'd been airborne for an hour. I was having so much fun I'd lost track of time.

When I had ten hours of solo in the P-40, I was ready for my final flight test – a one-hour flight with an evaluation pilot in the AT-6. Before we took off, he told me he would be grading me on my competence in flying the aircraft and my ability to react to instructions. As the tower cleared us for takeoff, he said, "Once we're airborne, please follow my instructions carefully. Going northwest, climb to six thousand feet, level off, and increase speed enough to do a regular loop. At the top of the loop do a snap one-half roll, make a sharp turn to the left, pull it into a stall, and let it spin out. At three thousand feet, pull out of the spin. If you've done all of that correctly, I'll probably be asleep so wake me up and I'll give you new instructions."

As I completed the final maneuver he said, "Turn south to the auxiliary field and perform the following landings: left front wheel, right front wheel, and three-point. Then, traveling first east and then west, land cross wind in each direction. In all cases, when you have touched down, you will not roll out. Apply power and take off again."

After the last landing in the series, I had climbed to about one thousand feet when the engine quit – the instructor had shut it down. I put the nose down, turned sharply to the left, and, leaving the flaps up, put the wheels down. I reached the field with about a hundred yards to spare. On instruction, I cranked the engine and went airborne again. The rest of the test flight was more of the same and finally the instructor said, "Please take us home."

I was tired but pleased with myself. I was sure I had passed, but my instructor didn't prepare me for the next comment. In front of several other students gathered around the AT-6 he said, "Gentlemen, I just had an airplane ride." As I left, I thanked him for the comment and he said, "My pleasure." As I recall, I was walking about two feet above the ground.

Two days later in a ceremony attended by my proud mother and Mrs. Mansur, I was pinned with silver wings and gold bars. Later that day I received my orders. I was to proceed to Tallahassee, Florida, a holding base, to await further orders assigning me to a fighter base for final combat training before being shipped to a combat zone and assigned to a fighter squadron. The fact that I was going to the east coast meant that I would in all probability be assigned to a fighter squadron in the European Theatre and that was good news to me.

IV

P-51 MUSTANG –
"THE RED-NOSED BOYS"

The thing that impressed me the most during the long and tedious train ride from Phoenix to Tallahassee was the courtesy, helpfulness, and gratitude of the American people towards men in uniform. I don't believe a day went by that I wasn't patted on the back several times and told, "Thank you and go with God." It made me proud to serve.

I thought that I would only be in Tallahassee for a few days but, with the limited training facilities and the huge build up in our Armed Forces, including fighter pilots, it turned out to be nearly six weeks. We didn't train or really do anything militarily; we just waited – an unlikely combination of boredom and anxiety.

Finally, on January 12, 1944, I received orders to report to Bartow Air Base, Florida, for my final combat training. Bartow was a P-51 base. I was ecstatic! I would be flying our most advanced fighter aircraft – the already famous Mustang.

My first flight in the P-51 exceeded all expectations. I had been told by other pilots of its enormous power and maneuverability, but when I pushed that throttle forward for the first time, and roared down the runway and into the sky, I knew I had a winner. I felt that the Mustang and I were one, and together we were going to be invincible. A fellow pilot, in a letter to his sister, described the impressions I took away from that first flight in the P-51:

"... At 1305 I climbed into the cockpit of a P-51 and at 1321 I pushed the throttle forward and went <u>blasting</u> down the runway on my first flight. I have never flown an <u>airplane</u> until today. The past 1200 or so hours I've spent in the air were just spent loafing along. When I say that I went blasting down the runway, I'm not kidding. It's the first

airplane I've flown that accelerates so fast that my head was thrown back against the headrest. It leaves the ground at a mere 110 mph and eats up altitude like a homesick angel. This plane is everything I've heard it is and even more. To put it in a few choice words, this is a pilot's airplane. You can do things in this job with one finger on the stick that would take two hands in any other plane. The man (or men) that designed this P-51 ought to get a large medal. I'm spoiled now. I won't want to fly any other plane."

As soon as we were checked out and had a few hours to become familiar with the P-51, we started training in combat tactics. This mostly consisted of gaining a position on the tail of another aircraft (called a "rabbit") and keeping your gun sights on him and at the same time evading another aircraft that was trying to do the same to you. Former combat pilots who knew all the tricks flew the "rabbit" aircraft.

One evening at the Officers Club, a Captain with combat experience told me how to do a certain maneuver that would not only shake an enemy on your tail, but would also put you behind him. A couple of days later, when I was being pursued and flying at about four hundred miles per hour, I put my P-51 into this maneuver and, though I wasn't quite sure how it happened, I wound up behind my pursuer. The aircraft didn't feel right when I landed. I later learned that the maneuver had thrown the frame of the aircraft some two degrees off normal. The aircraft was grounded and I was told not to try that maneuver again unless it was a real matter of life and death.

In addition to dogfighting, we practiced aerial gunnery and did quite a lot of night flying. This was particularly challenging when it was overcast and you couldn't see the horizon, or much of anything else for that matter. Some months later, when flying through the heavy overcasts of Europe, we would be very thankful for this training.

Saturday nights at Bartow were always a fun time because, like at Tallahassee, some of the local young ladies would join us at the Officers Club for dining and dancing. It was at one of these functions that I met a pretty southern belle who would later become part of my life.

A week before my class was to graduate and be shipped overseas I broke the little finger on my right hand while playing volleyball. There were no doctors on base so I was taken to a local doctor who set the bone, put a cast on the finger, and told me to come back in a month. This wouldn't have been such a big deal except that, as a result, I was taken off of flying status, my orders for shipment overseas were cancelled and I was reassigned to "temporary duty for administrative purposes" at Bartow. When a month had gone by the doctor removed the cast. The fracture had healed but the joint was frozen - the little finger stuck straight out. So, to my great frustration, my shipping orders were delayed again.

I was sent to Drew Field in Tampa, forty miles away, for evaluation by an orthopedic surgeon. He decided that I should come every day for a Jacuzzi and massage treatment until the joint became mobile again. The only Jacuzzi there was a regular people-size so I would have to kneel and stick my finger in for fifteen minutes and then get it massaged. This went on for a couple of weeks. The first week, someone had to fly me there and back each day. After that I was told to fly myself so I was placed back on flight status.

When I wasn't going back and forth to Tampa, I continued to perform administrative duties. I spent a lot of time flight-testing repaired aircraft and flying "rabbit" for training purposes. One day, while flight-testing a P-51 that had undergone major repair, I was flying over a heavy overcast that extended from about two thousand feet up to nine thousand feet. I was at fifteen thousand feet when two descending aircraft shot by, one on either side of me, and pulled up about a thousand feet below. Startled, I went to full throttle and rolled left to take a look. They were two Navy F4Fs and I gathered that they were looking to see what a P-51 could do and I was more than glad to show them. For the next thirty minutes or so we had a great dogfight in which I believe they gained some respect for the faster and more maneuverable Mustang. Unfortunately, I was having so much fun showing off that I had paid no mind to direction or distance. Finally, I realized that I was getting low on fuel so I waggled my wings and peeled off to head home. But the ceiling had dropped dramatically and when I broke through the bottom, I was at four hundred feet over water with no land in sight.

It quickly dawned on me that I was in trouble. I had taken all the navigation courses and, in fact, had done quite well on paper, but in actual flight, I had found that the best navigation aids were rivers, railroad tracks, or highways. I figured that if the weather wasn't good enough to see these things, then I should stay on the ground. Since I had done most of my flying over the desert, under sunny skies, this premise had not been disabused. But I wasn't over the desert now and the skies weren't sunny and I was in a pickle.

I tried my radio but could not pick up any response. That left me with only one choice. The P-51 had a receiver that picked up a directional beam that was transmitted from different airfields around the country. I turned on the receiver and spun the dial. Nothing! I tried several more times without success. I could feel my stomach starting to churn. Then suddenly I picked up the didi-dot-didi and tuned in on it; all beams were broadcast from mainland stations and that's where I wanted to go, and quickly. I was flying east and the signal was getting stronger, so I knew that I was over the Gulf of Mexico heading for the west coast of Florida. A quick calculation indicated that I had at best fifteen to sixteen minutes of flying time before I ran out of fuel. I gave an involuntary shudder as I thought about the possibility of going into the Gulf. I never was a good swimmer; I didn't particularly like the ocean, and I certainly didn't fancy floating around in the Gulf, even in a life-preserver. Besides, I figured that if I augured in, I'd end up with more than a broken finger.

As these gloomy thoughts were about to overtake me, I looked up from my instrument panel and, glory be, where the overcast met the horizon, I could see land. As I passed over the coastline, I spotted a small airfield. There was no tower to ask for landing instructions or wind direction so I aimed straight at the runway and brought that Mustang down like a baby carriage. I let it roll to the end of the runway and sat there for some minutes composing myself. Finally, I peered upward towards the dark ceiling and said aloud, "God, I can't handle too many challenges like this!" A little voice, which sounded much like my own, replied, "Then learn to navigate!"

As I shut the engine down, a fire truck approached and two firemen jumped out. One of them came over and asked if I needed assistance. I said, "Yes, gasoline." The fireman shook his head. "The nearest gasoline for your airplane is a hundred and fifty miles away. I'll make a call, but I'm sure they won't be able to get it here before tomorrow morning." He added that they would be leaving in about an hour and that the airfield would be closed.

I considered my limited options: my air base was about two hundred miles away, no fuel available until morning, I had no money, no checking account, and no identification save my dog tags and silver wings. I asked the firemen if they would give me a ride into the nearby town I'd seen when I was coming in. They said, "Sure." They dropped me off at what I believe was the only motel in the small town of Suwanee, Florida. In the front office, which doubled as tavern, I explained my dilemma to the night manager-bartender. Two men sitting at the bar piped up that they had seen me land. In yet another show of the American mood, the manager not only gave me a room, he also allowed me to write a check for thirty dollars on a plain sheet of paper against my mother's account at her bank in Los Angeles. I was so moved and thankful I bought a round for the bar – all four of us. When my new friend poured the drinks I noticed that he used Canadian Club and Johnnie Walker Red Label. He charged me fifty cents a drink. I was quite surprised because good liquor was hard to come by in those days, particularly around military bases. At Bartow, we were used to drinking a mediocre brand of whisky, and paying some twelve dollars a bottle. I swallowed the whisky and my pride and asked him if he had enough on hand to sell me a few bottles. He said he had plenty. They had expected an air base to be built nearby and he had put in a large supply. When it turned out that all they got was the emergency landing strip, he was stuck with it. My cash on hand bought me six bottles of Canadian Club – the check was approved and paid.

The next morning the firemen picked me up on their way to the airfield. Shortly after we arrived a tanker showed up and fueled my aircraft. My problem now was getting the liquor home. The cockpit of a P-51 was not designed to carry anything but the pilot. But since it was a short flight, about forty minutes, and the stakes were high, I figured I could manage. I stuck two bottles on my lap and squeezed two on each side of me, did a quick pre-flight, waved to the firemen, and roared off, hoping that I wouldn't run into turbulent weather that might cause some of my precious cargo to break.

As soon as I was airborne, I called home base to inform them that I was enroute and would call for landing instructions in about twenty minutes. I landed and as I taxied to my parking place, I spotted the Colonel waiting for me. I thought, "Oh boy, now I'm in for it."

The Colonel, not looking too happy, jumped up on the wing before I had even shut the engine down. As I opened the canopy, he looked down and it was obvious that he spotted my cargo. He stood there gaping for a few moments and then simply said, "Glad you're back. After you're debriefed, stop by my office." I felt like the little boy caught with his fingers in the cookie jar wondering how bad the spanking was going to be.

An hour later I reported to the Colonel, heels locked, ramrod straight, and with my sharpest salute. He told me to stand at ease and tell him what had happened. I explained as briefly as I could: the chance meeting with the Navy fighters, the dogfight, ending up low on fuel over the Gulf and having to follow a beam to the emergency field, and finally having to wait overnight for fuel.

He listened without comment and when I was finished asked only two questions. "How did the dogfight go?" and "Where did you get the liquor and do they have any more?" I told him that the dogfight had gone very well and that I believed that there was more liquor where that came from. The Colonel nodded and looked thoughtful for a moment and then said, "Lieutenant Achen, I think you need to get checked out in the C-78. I'll check you out personally. Be ready to take off at 1400." Thus, by a stroke of good fortune and a mutual esteem for good whisky, the Colonel and I became friends.

During the latter days of training at Bartow, I had dated, courted and fallen in love with Barbara, a lovely southern belle from Winterhaven, Florida. In those war years, millions of young men, like me, had to make many complex decisions way beyond our years and life experience. One of the toughest, and the one I now faced, was whether to get married now, before shipping out, or wait until I returned... if I returned... when the war was over. This was not a simple yes or no proposition. There were the emotional aspects – Did I really love her? – Did she really love me? – Was it fair to her to ask her to marry me given the uncertainties we both faced?

But maybe more thorny than the emotional, were the practical considerations. I had to get permission from my Commanding Officer and, if Barbara said yes, I had to find a place for her to live while I was gone. We were in Florida and I wanted to return to and live in California when the war was over. I had to resolve these problems before I could even ask her to marry me. The logistics were quickly resolved. I called my mother in Los Angeles, explained the situation to her and asked if I could send my intended bride out to live with her until I returned. Without hesitation, she said, "Certainly. What is her name and when will she arrive?"

That done, I went to see the Colonel. He gave the required permission, and told me that if I wanted to apply for instructor duty at Bartow, he would give it full consideration. I thanked him, but respectfully declined. From the time I was sworn in, it had been my dream, and I truly believed my destiny, to be a fighter pilot in combat. Nothing would change that!

I asked Barbara to marry me and she said, "Yes." I asked her if she would go and live with my mother in Los Angeles when I shipped out and again she said, "Yes" but asked if she could take her sister, Vivian, with her. I knew it would be okay with my mother so I agreed.

We were married two weeks later in a lovely church wedding. All I can remember was the packed church and the many flowers. A short honeymoon in Tampa and we returned to Bartow to get packed and for me to get ready to go overseas. Bob Miller, another P-51 pilot, was to go with me to New York where we reported to the Overseas Transportation Office.

We were quartered at the Chesterfield Hotel and we were told to call a certain telephone number at 8 o'clock each night until we received orders. For several nights, we called in and were told to call again the next night. On the fourth or fifth call we were told to have our bags packed and that a car would pick us up in an hour. We were picked up and taken to La Guardia Field where, after a two hour wait, we were told that the flight had been cancelled. We were driven back to Manhattan, but this time we were put up at the Waldorf-Astoria – quite an upgrade!

The next night we were picked up again and this time the flight was on. We boarded a DC-4, which was packed to capacity, mostly with high-ranking officers. We flew from La Guardia to an airfield in Iceland where we spent several hours on the ground while the aircraft was serviced and then on to Ireland. The flight was long and I was exhausted when we arrived; between the pitching and rolling of the airplane in turbulence over the North Sea and the excitement of going to my combat assignment, I slept hardly at all.

After two days in Ireland, Bob Miller and I were flown to Glasgow, Scotland. There, we boarded a train bound for our final destination – Debden Air Base, England, home of the 4th Fighter Group. The 4th Fighter Group had evolved from the famous "Eagle Squadron." The noses of the P-51s flown by the 4th were all painted red. Thus, the Group came to be known to the Luftwaffe as "The Red-Nosed Boys." In an excerpt from "The Interrogator," Hanns Scharff talks about them:

"Any history written about the U.S. Army Air Forces in World War II would be incomplete if the Eagle Squadron remained unmentioned. These "Red-Nosed Boys" of "Double Winged" fame had become the 4th Fighter Group at Debden, England, in General Jess Auto's 5th Wing in the 8th Fighter Command. They were such a proud outfit that one of

*them who became our guest wrote a postcard from prison to his C.O.,
saying, "They know all about us over here, Boss, and they respect us.
Paint 'em ALL RED, Sir!" (He meant that the P-51s should be <u>all</u> red)"*

334 Squadron
4th Fighter
Group, bottom
row, 3rd from
left Norm Achen

1. Shot down Aug. 15, 1944   2. Solitary Confinement and
                                Interrogation
3. Stalag Luft 3   4. Spremberg   5. Nurenberg
6. Bavarian Alps   7. Patton   8. Nancy France

V

JUDGE, JURY, AND EXECUTIONER

D + 14 - Wednesday, June 23, 1944, Somewhere over Normandy

We had taken off from Debden at 0600 and, flying due east, had crossed over the rugged coast of Normandy without incident. The sky was clear and visibility hampered only by the clouds of smoke and dust rising from the battlefield. We were awed by the magnitude of the Allied invasion force hammering its way inland below us.

The squadron mission was to interdict enemy movement west toward the advancing Allied forces. This meant strafing anything that moved: Trains, trucks, tactical vehicles, and anything else that looked menacing. We had thus far detected no Luftwaffe presence over the operational area, so for now we had a free hand. We flew about fifteen hundred feet above the ground in a loose but disciplined formation, with individual and, sometimes, several aircraft peeling off to engage targets of opportunity and then rejoining the formation.

On this morning, we were ten or fifteen miles forward of our troops. My radio squelch broke, "Left flank, that's a German staff car pulling into the roadhouse, nine o'clock. Take it out." Left flank, that was me. "Roger."

I had spotted the car three or four miles ahead and about a mile to my left. At first, I wasn't sure it was a military vehicle, but anticipating, I had dropped my wing tanks and switched on my guns. At the order to engage, I rolled left and began a steep dive. At eight hundred feet, I had a perfect sight picture on the German staff car. I squeezed off a long burst and watched the tracers go directly into the target. Three German soldiers leaped from the car into a lethal storm of fifty-caliber gunfire.

47

They began twitching and jerking in what seemed a macabre dance around the now-burning vehicle – and then they lay dead on the ground. Dead! I had killed them. In those few moments I had become judge, jury, and executioner. I had willfully taken the lives of three human beings about whom I knew nothing. I was stunned. For a moment, I had target frustration that almost took me into the ground. At the last second, I pulled up and, as tiles peeled off the building in front of me, I realized I hadn't released the trigger. I barely cleared the building and vomited into my oxygen mask. I tore off the mask and promptly sprayed the cockpit with what was left in my stomach. Sweat was running down my neck and arms and I was shaking violently. I knew my mission was over for today. I had to get the aircraft home while I could.

"Eagle One, this is Red Dog. Request permission to abort and head for home."

"Red Dog, go ahead. Do you need escort?"

"Negative, out."

I don't remember much about the flight home. I later learned that two planes from the squadron flew escort for me. One of the escort pilots told me that I followed the correct procedures for the situation. I hit the deck, throttled to emergency boost and headed for the channel. I wasn't thinking about it - I just did it.

As I made my way back over the channel I stopped shaking and my stomach seemed to stabilize. I reflected. I had just experienced two new events in my life. One I initiated, the other was the result. The humiliation and self-doubt would soon go away – the act of gunning down three human beings would not.

Oddly, it was my reaction that bothered me most as I headed in. I had been flying for four years and, at twenty-three, I was totally confident in my ability as a pilot. I had done everything any plane I had flown was designed and equipped to do and beyond. I was, as an aviator, without fear and yet I'd momentarily come apart. I was wearing and surrounded by the repulsive evidence.

As I started my descent into Debden, I was trying to figure out how I could avoid my crew chiefs and clean up the mess myself. Maybe they wouldn't be there when I landed. Not likely!

Any hope of slipping in unnoticed vanished when I got my landing instructions from the tower:

"Red Dog, this is Debden Tower. Come straight in on runway ten L."

Reluctantly, "Red Dog. Roger ten L."

Damn, they were giving me priority – I'd been had.

The next communication came as I was taxiing. "Red Dog, this is tower. Proceed straight away to your parking area."

I taxied to the parking area, shut down, and cranked the canopy back, all the while wishing I could disappear. I should have had more faith in the professionalism of my crew. My crew chiefs reached down to help me out of the cockpit: No smiles, no smirks, no expressions of pity, just business. I was thankful but all I could respond with was a subdued, "Sorry."

As if rehearsed, both men answered in unison, "No big deal, Lieutenant." And then one said, "The jeep is waiting to take you to your quarters." That meant we were bypassing the ready room where, after every mission, there was a debriefing, a parachute check, and often a shot of rye. I could have used the shot of rye.

I took a long shower, at first with my flight suit on. Then I stripped down and sat on the floor under a jet of warm water. I washed away the corruption on my clothes and body but I couldn't cleanse my mind. I had done what I had been trained to do. No more, no less. But as I sat there on that shower floor, I realized that I had not been mentally prepared for the personal involvement in the taking of human life.

As I was getting dressed, there was a knock on the door. That would be the Chaplain.

"May I come in?"

I wanted to tell him to go away. I needed time to work through this. But I answered, "Yes."

The Padre sat next to me on the bed. He was a gaunt man of indeterminate age – could have been thirty-five or sixty. He had deep-set, sad eyes that looked like they had seen it all. We sat silent for a time and then the Chaplain asked softly, "Can you tell me about it?"

At that moment I could not. I shook my head.

We were silent again. I guess I was angry at the intrusion. What could he know about what I was going through? Then, I asked, "Chaplain, have you ever killed a man?"

He put his hands gently on my shoulders, looked straight into my eyes and said quietly, "No, my son, but that's not my mission."

Then the Chaplain, knowing that our conversation was over for now, said, "We'll speak again when you're ready." And with that he left me with my demons.

VI

MIRACLES

MONDAY, August 15

From a distance, I could hear the phone ringing. Awareness came slowly. The phone was still ringing, closer now, and urgent. I picked it up in mid-ring.

"Yes," very softly.

A tentative, "Lieutenant?"

"Yes."

"The Colonel wants to know if you can fly today."

As I looked at my watch... 0630... I thought, what a silly question, if the Colonel wants me to fly, I fly.

Then it occurred to me that my squadron wasn't supposed to fly today. Our schedules never wavered. Days off were considered sacred. Something out of the ordinary was going down.

"Lieutenant?"

"Yes, sure I'll fly. What's up?"

"I don't know, sir. Briefing room at 0800, please."

Through the window, I could see the first light and rare blush of color over the gray English countryside. I went to the window and, as I did first thing every morning, looked skyward. It was clear - the last stars were blinking out. Chances are it would be clear over the continent, too. A mixed blessing. Fog and clouds were welcome when you needed to "disappear," but were dicey for takeoff and landing. In bad weather, such as fog or heavy rain, two planes would take off together – plane one on instruments, and plane two struggling to stay three feet off plane one's wingtip. In this manner, the squadron could rise above the weather, circle until all aircraft were in formation, and head for the designated target area. Coming home in bad weather was another matter. We could only hope that a Higher Power would part the clouds and guide us in. If not, we had to look for another airfield that was clear enough to land on. Not easy and not fun.

I showered, shaved, and dressed. My head ached from too much partying and too little sleep. My rear end was still sore from a long unscheduled mission we had flown three days before when a convoy of German supply ships had been spotted off the coast of Norway. A squadron of British torpedo bombers was assigned to take them out but the Brits didn't have any long range fighters available for escort, so we were asked to help out. The flight over the North Sea was particularly stressful. We had stayed no more than twenty-five feet above the water in order to avoid detection by German radar. Flying at twenty-five feet for three hours is like being in a cage with hungry lions – if you don't maintain total concentration, you're going to get eaten.

When we reached the convoy, we climbed to ten thousand feet and watched the torpedo bombers go to work. They sank at least twelve ships and I saw several more on fire. We stayed with the bombers until they were out of danger from the Luftwaffe and then hightailed it for home at a much better altitude.

After a few hours, the seat of a Mustang begins to feel like cement, and the tight configuration of the cockpit makes it impossible to change positions. Now I wished that I had taken time to find our flight surgeon and get his famous "Doc Randle's four pill cure-all" for whatever ailment. But absent that, I was hoping today's mission would be no more than three or four hours and I could handle that.

I passed on breakfast and had coffee and a fresh donut in the ready room. I walked into the briefing room, took a seat in the front row, and awaited the briefing officer. The young Lions were unusually quiet and subdued. I think we all sensed that today was going to be different. I'd been a combat pilot for over two months now, and had yet to see, let alone engage, an enemy aircraft. Since D-Day, we'd done massive strafing in France. When the Allied invasion force was well established and moving east, our mission had changed. We had started flying escort for the strategic bombers going in to pound military and industrial targets deep in the heart of the "Fatherland." These escort missions had taken us to all parts of Germany that our range allowed, even to the coast of Norway, but we had not engaged or even seen the vaunted Luftwaffe.

Six weeks had passed since the strafing incident. I was still having the nightmare, but less frequently, and, like most of my young fellow warriors, I'd done a lot of growing up in the last two months. As a combat pilot I was much tougher and more confident. I was ready for the ultimate test – aerial combat; not man to man but fighter to fighter; the Mustang against the Messerschmitt – it wasn't personal. No one painted men on their aircraft, only airplanes. Success was measured by how many enemy planes you could shoot down.

When the briefing officer entered the room, I noticed that his expression was uncharacteristically grim. Others must have noticed too, because the room became very quiet, expectant.

The briefing began... "Gentlemen, this morning while you were sleeping, Allied forces launched an invasion into southern France. That is why the squadron is flying today. The objective is to tie up German assets and thus divert their attention away from the invasion area." He then briefed us on our specific mission. We were to rendezvous with the B-24s at a point on the western border of Germany and escort them to their target area in northern Germany. Then the squadron would split - half escorting the bombers home, and the other half flying search-and-destroy strafing missions back through Germany and France to the Allied lines.

We were all excited as we picked up our parachutes, survival kits, and additional formation instructions and were driven to our aircraft. The P-51s were parked, each in its own enforcement, spread out over the field to prevent a one-strike knockout. Crew chiefs had engines running. We taxied into line and took off two abreast.

We headed for the continent in close formation, flying at about ten thousand feet. As we approached the French coastline, we climbed to twenty-three thousand and spread out into combat formation. Shortly after that, we came under heavy ground fire. Anti-aircraft bursts sent deadly clouds of shrapnel into the air around us; each burst capable of downing an aircraft. This was a huge problem for the bombers, but the fighters were able to climb quickly out of range.

We had been well trained, both in classroom briefings and in the sky, on what to do in various emergency situations. Emergency procedures became ingrained. One of the things pounded into us was to become familiar with the continental coastline so that if we got separated from the squadron we could find our way home. As I studied the rugged Normandy beaches this day, it didn't enter my mind that it might be my last look at the French coast for months to come.

Making our way east toward Germany, my thoughts were more on what lay ahead and above. The Luftwaffe! Was I ready to take them on? We regularly took to the air in mock dogfights and I had confidence in my ability as a fighter pilot and was confident that my Mustang was superior to the German ME 109. But the Luftwaffe was not to be dismissed lightly; they had vast experience against the Russians and the British, and their daring and tenacity in battle was legendary. Rumor had it that when a Luftwaffe pilot was downed, he was miraculously rescued and given a new plane to fly and fight another day.

We rendezvoused with the B-24s as planned near the German border. Flying about two thousand feet above the bombers, we watched helpless as they disappeared into a giant cloud of flak. I held my breath – moments later all of them came lumbering out undamaged on the other side of the deadly shrapnel field. Amazing!

As I watched them fly bravely on toward their target, I thought about these giant airplanes and their crews and considered their chances of surviving this war. I knew that the loss of sixty bombers on a given day was not unusual. Each with a crew of ten, that was six hundred souls committed to God. These were America's finest - eager, excited boys who had become men in the clouds of flak and the rattling of machine gun fire high above the earth. They came with a patriotic fervor that soon turned into a realization that war, or at least the war that they knew, was truly hell, full of unspeakable horror and terrifying apparitions that would forever torment those who were lucky enough to survive.

And if the crew of a doomed bomber successfully parachuted, chances are they would quickly be captured by German soldiers or Hitler Youth and turned over to SS troopers, or the Gestapo. Either way, their chances of reaching a POW camp were slim. From what I'd been told, physical and mental torture was the usual outcome. There was no telling how many had been executed or otherwise died in captivity. I shuddered involuntarily as I thought of American airmen in the hands of the Nazi monsters.

My grim reverie was broken with the squelch of the radio. The squadron commander ordered half the squadron, including me, to drop down to strafing level and to fly west towards the coast seeking out and destroying targets of opportunity; i.e., anything capable of transporting men or equipment to the front.

Descending to about six hundred feet, the squadron headed west in loose formation. I swung about a mile or so to the south where I spotted a locomotive partially hidden in the woods with just the engine jutting out. Steam rose from the engine's stack and I could not detect any armament. Out of the corner of my eye, I vaguely noticed a small village nearby but my senses focused on the train. My breathing almost came to a stop as I slowed to two hundred knots and rolled in on the target, activating the gun switch and sighting the guns. As I prepared to pull the trigger, the Mustang shook violently. Lord Almighty, I had been hit! As the message got through to my consciousness, I became aware of a sharp burning in my right leg, and as my oxygen mask and goggles flew off, a sharp stinging in my forehead. Then there was a profound silence. My engine had quit.

At that moment, training and reflexes took control. I cranked the canopy back but realized that I was too low for the parachute to open. I'd have to ride her in. I nosed the Mustang towards an open space that I had seen, or maybe sensed, before I was hit. The clearing was a tiny open area, not three hundred yards long, surrounded by tall trees and dotted with boulders. It gave me little hope of survival, but I was dropping fast, and had run out of options. I could only give it a go and hope.

Blood from somewhere was getting into my eyes, hampering my vision. I mopped my face with my sleeve. Focus! I had to focus! Slipping the plane to the left, I barely cleared the trees. Fighting to control the aircraft with my right hand, I threw my left arm around the gun sights to protect my head. I'd done all I could do. I closed my eyes and murmured, "It's all yours, God."

Fighter pilots have a reputation for arrogance. Indeed, we are not a humble lot, and that's the truth. But at that moment, I knew that if I survived this one, it would not be through my skill and dexterity. I needed Divine Intervention – a Miracle.

I remember little about what happened in the next few minutes: surreal – gliding – opened my eyes – windshield covered with blood – must be mine – to my right, a boulder – wing slices through it – amazing – plane spinning – ground spinning – darkness – silence.

Some one was shouting. Very close – I opened one eye and promptly closed it again. I was alive! I was lying on my back in a grassy field. I don't know how I got there. I would reflect more on that later, but right now I had a problem. Close to the side of my head was the barrel of what appeared to be an old muzzle-loading rifle, in the hands of an old angry farmer. He was shouting in German and pointing the rifle alternately at my head and at the field behind me. It finally got across that my plane had killed three of his cows – those weren't boulders after all. I guessed that explaining that it wasn't my fault, that God had been at the controls, would not have helped my case.

This bad situation got worse. Three pitchfork-brandishing youths appeared. I got the uneasy feeling that they wanted to take control of my capture, or perhaps my execution. For the first time I felt real fear. I knew without a doubt that if these men got their hands on me I was in terrible trouble.

The small crowd grew, in numbers, volume, and intensity – several other people arrived, most looked like farmers, some with wives. Everyone was talking loudly in German, apparently arguing about my future, or lack thereof. At some point during this loud debate, the world began to spin again and I lost consciousness. Sometime later, I don't know how much time had passed, I became aware of a female voice speaking in English.

A young girl, maybe twelve or so, was peering into my face and gesturing toward an older woman, "She wants you to come with her. Can you get up?" Although there were angry, hostile faces all around, the sound of this wisp of a girl speaking my own language gave me hope. Was she an angel? Was I about to become a part of Miracle number two? I began to believe that maybe I would not die today, in this little field, in this foreign land, at the hands of these angry people.

She spoke again, "Do you need help?"

I shook my head. Whatever my fate, whatever my fears, I would go with dignity. I struggled to get up but my right leg collapsed in pain. I muffled a cry and gritted my teeth. Someone, a woman I think, reached to help me up, but one of the men pushed her away. I struggled to my feet and nodded that I was ready - for what, I had no idea.

I walked between the girl and the older woman. Apparently the older woman had overruled the young thugs and I was in the custody of these women. But the farmers followed close behind with their ancient weapons trained on my back. If I'd had the energy or inclination to escape, it quickly vanished. I couldn't run and I couldn't hide. I stayed close to the women.

The young girl asked my name, indicating that the other woman wanted to know. I told her my name, but only that. The older woman said something and the girl translated that I was being taken to a farmhouse where the proper authorities would be notified of my capture. Her English had a soothing effect on me. I asked how she came to speak my language. She told me that it was a required subject at school. Latin had been required at my school – bloody lot of good that did me now. I sensed that my immediate salvation lay in the hands of this Fraulein. I had a Zippo lighter in my pocket, a precious item in the war years. I gave it to "Fraulein," as she will always be known to me. She smiled shyly and said, "Thank you." I didn't have the presence of mind to ask her name but, to this day, I am grateful for the part she played in my salvation.

When we arrived at the farmhouse, the women, followed by the victimized farmer, escorted me through a heavy wooden door into the kitchen. The rest of the crowd waited outside either, I supposed, out of curiosity or in hopes of being recognized as part of the capturing force. While the farmer was calling to report my capture, I was seated at the table, given a greatly appreciated cup of steaming coffee and a warm wet cloth to clean the blood from my forehead, leg and several other minor wounds that I discovered. My head was throbbing and I ached everywhere but, compared to my overall predicament, this seemed insignificant.

As I sat, the woman left the room, returning shortly with a small oval portrait of a young man. Through Fraulein I learned that he was her only child. He'd been killed in the war. She didn't say where or when and I wondered if she blamed me. I tried to tell her how sorry I was. Her loss and her tears touched me deeply. I turned away to hide my own.

I was taken outside to await "the authorities." When they came to take me away, I turned to catch the eyes of Fraulein, to say without words how her kindness had helped me and given me hope. But the three figures were slowly returning to the farmhouse. I would think of this time often in the months and years to come.

My "car" was some kind of mutant contraption powered by a mixture of coal and wood. It occurred to me that there would be precious little petrol available in these lean times. I was driven to a city that was heavily damaged, I assumed from aerial bombardment. I suspected it was Hanover, but since my escorts weren't very friendly or talkative, I didn't think it prudent to ask. My captors pulled me out of the car and took me into a building that appeared to be a maximum-security type prison. I was shoved roughly into a windowless cell that was perhaps eight by ten feet. A bare bulb that gave off precious little light hung from the ceiling. The only furnishing was a crude wooden bench, which apparently was to serve as my bed.

My G.I. wristwatch had quit working and I was unable to judge the time but several hours must have elapsed before I had my first visitor, a burly, unpleasant man with a bad odor and a bad attitude. He performed a full body search, then took my watch and left. Shortly after that, a doctor or nurse came in and inspected and minimally treated my wounds. This would be the only medical attention I would receive.

The burly guard brought my dinner (or lunch or breakfast - I wasn't sure). It was some type of concoction that smelled and tasted like barley along with vile black bread that tasted a lot like wood shavings. I later learned that it was indeed made with a generous amount of sawdust. Its sour, foul taste nauseated me and after one bite, which I spit out, I hurled it into a dark corner. I downed the soup and a cup of cold weak coffee. I made a bed of the wooden bench and lay down. I wondered how long it had been since the phone at Debden awakened me. Maybe eighteen hours. This mission turned out to be a bit more complicated than the three- or four-hour flight that I'd anticipated. My world had changed dramatically in these several hours. I had no doubt that I was in the most important and dangerous time of my life, however long that may be. With that thought, I fell into a merciful sleep.

I awoke in a cold sweat, shaking uncontrollably. I knew that events had caught up with me and I was in a sort of delayed shock. I almost cried out, but my dulled, frightened senses told me that there was no one on this earth that I could call to for help. Not my mother, father, brother, or friends. I was scared and near despair. Only God could help me now.

But I knew that for God to help me, I had to help myself. I had to stand up and take charge of my own fate, regain my wits and my self-respect. I was an Officer in the United States Army – my mission, the mission of every American Prisoner of War, was to survive and escape. The first order was to survive.

I was excited now - the shaking and sweats were gone. I paced back and forth in my cell, looking for inspiration. It came to me in words from Dylan Thomas that I had been required to memorize when I was a student at Elgin Academy in Illinois: "Go not gentle into that good night – rage, rage against the dying of the light." These words would become my driving force, my rallying cry. I was going to survive. I was certain that God had already brought me through the crash and the pitchforks. Surely He would not leave me now.

Suddenly the disgusting piece of bread that I had tossed in the corner became a symbol of survival. I needed to stay strong. I recovered the bread and choked it down. I had new determination. I would not go gentle!

It was later that day when my cell door opened and two German soldiers entered. One spoke to me in English. He said that they were taking me to Frankfurt.

The light hurt my eyes as we came out of the semi-darkness of my cell onto a busy street. From the position of the sun, I judged it to be late afternoon. As they walked me to the train station, a hostile crowd gathered and followed us. In my now tattered and dirty uniform, I'm sure they had no doubt that I was an American, probably one who had rained bombs down on them. They began to shout and spit at me. I didn't respond. I kept my shoulders straight and my head high. An elderly, well-dressed man stepped up and hit me several times with his cane. I took the blows without flinching or raising my arms in defense. I met the old man's eyes and he turned and walked away muttering to himself. Apparently that impressed the guards; they pushed the crowd back and protected me from further contact.

Upon boarding the train, I was directed to take an aisle seat near the back of the car. I was down to one guard now and he took a seat across the aisle from me. A man in a dark suit came into the car and took a seat behind me. I paid him no mind at the time, but shortly after the train started moving I received an eye-rotating blow to the head, followed by a stream of German invective. I covered to fend off further assault but the guard spoke sharply to the man and he left me alone after that.

As the hours passed I thought about home and family. I knew that by now my wife and my mom would have been notified that I was missing in action, and they would be overcome with grief. I hoped that they would soon be notified that I was a prisoner of war, so they would at least know that I was alive, but I didn't know whether that system worked or not. I said a prayer for them.

The soldier touching my arm and telling me that we were getting off broke my reverie. The train screeched and jerked to a stop and we exited. As it was late at night, there were only a few people on the platform, for which I was grateful. They stared but did not bother me. We walked several blocks and entered what appeared to be an old vacant warehouse. We descended some very steep steps into a dimly-lit dirt sort of basement. Then I saw these enormous casks and realized that it was an old wine cellar. The guard chained me to one of the steel supports and, without so much as a word or a backward glance, ascended the stairs and was gone. The air was cool and damp. It was mid-summer, but here in my dungeon there was no warmth. Sometime later, the guard re-entered the cellar and, from the strong odor of alcohol and tobacco on him, I guessed that he was having more fun than I was. He brought me black bread and lukewarm coffee, but no blankets.

Early the next morning we boarded another train. We had been briefed that, if captured, we would be taken to Frankfurt to the central POW interrogation center. As I anticipated, this was our destination. Information was that prisoners only spent two or three days there and were then shipped on to a permanent POW camp. Pretty routine.

In my case it was much more complicated – and life threatening.

VII

SOLITARY

"I regret to inform you that your husband, Norman W. Achen,
is missing in action as of 15 August 1944... "

These awful words from the War Department, intended for my wife,
were delivered to my stepfather, Grover Linn, at his place in Los Angeles
on 16 August 1944. My wife and mother were visiting in Tucson at the
time. This created a dilemma for my stepfather. He didn't want to call
them and convey this dreadful news over the telephone. Although he and
I had never gotten along well, he was a decent man and knew that he had
to deliver this terrible news personally.

Public transportation, trains, and busses were totally booked, mainly
moving soldiers and new recruits, so Grover decided to drive. This was
not an easy task for him to undertake. First, his driver's license had
been rescinded for some transgression or another, but the more pressing
problem was fuel. Gas was severely rationed in 1944 and Grover didn't
have enough gas coupons to get to Tucson, let alone back to Los Angeles.
But with the faith of a Baptist minister and the cunning of a lawyer, both
of which he had been at one time or another, Grover set out. He made
it as far as Yuma, Arizona, where, with the needle showing on empty
and no coupons, he pulled into a small roadside gas station. When the
attendant, who happened to be the owner, approached, Grover rolled
down the window and handed the telegram to him. He explained that
he was my father and that he was trying to get to Tucson to deliver the
tragic news personally to my wife and mother and that he had no more
coupons. The man, this stranger, this American by the wayside in Yuma,
Arizona, filled the tank and told my stepfather that if he needed gas on
the way home to stop in. He wouldn't let him pay. He then put his hand

on Grover's shoulder and said, "God bless you for what you're doing and God bless and protect your son." When my stepfather told me this story many months later, we both teared up and all I could think about was GOD BLESS AMERICA!

Frankfurt Interrogation Center, 18 August 1944

As soon as the door closed on my cell at the Frankfurt Interrogation Center, I began to take stock. Was escape possible? What was in the cell that would be useful to me? The cell was about six by eight feet with a high ceiling, maybe ten or twelve feet. A single bare light bulb hung from the ceiling. There was a wooden bunk covered with straw for a mattress, cantilevered from the wall; no legs to use as a club or pry bar. The walls and door were heavy plank. The door had a two- by four-inch view hole that opened from the outside allowing the guards to look in without opening the door. There was a small opaque window just below the ceiling and, below that, a heater. The light and the heater were both enclosed in heavy wire mesh and controlled from the guard station. There was one filthy blanket, a battered metal pitcher, and a tin can for drinking. No other utensils or movable objects that could be used for digging, gouging, cutting or stabbing. My assessment didn't leave me with much hope. The cell was clearly not meant to provide the occupant comfort, conveniences or means of escape.

The austerity of the facility and the lack of basic hygienic tools such as soap, tooth brush, and shaving gear reinforced my assumption, based on prior briefings, that I would only be here a couple of days. I paced the small cell trying to imagine what lay ahead. When I tired of that, I sat on the bed and awaited the interrogators. None came that day. I was allowed to go out to the bathroom and fill the water pitcher. I was not allowed to wash or brush my teeth. Sometime after the opaque window darkened, I lay down on the hard bunk and dozed fitfully. Two or three times during the night I heard the view hole open and close, but no one came in.

The next morning the guard escorted me to the toilet and again I was allowed to fill my water pitcher. Shortly after I was returned to my cell, the guard brought me a slice of black bread and a cup of ersatz coffee that tasted awful. Based on what I'd been told at Debden, I was sure that I'd soon be interrogated and shipped out. I was eager to get it over with.

But the day dragged on and no one came for me. My eagerness turned to mild anxiety. Around noon, the guard came back with another cup of the foul-tasting coffee. Repugnant as it was, I drank it. Then in the mid-afternoon, the cell door was opened and two of the guards stepped in. One said in broken English, "Is this the war criminal they're going to shoot?" That got my attention, but I sensed right away that it had to be staged. Why would they converse in English if not for my benefit? I wanted to say, "Oh, bullshit. Cut the crap and get on with the interrogation," but I remained silent and, I hoped, impassive. They stood there for a few moments watching for a reaction. Then the guard who hadn't spoken shrugged and said something in German and they closed the door and left. Mind games to scare me? I was pretty certain that was it unless killing cows was a war crime. I couldn't think of anything I'd done to warrant the charge. I wondered if they did this to all the POWs to soften them up for interrogation. I shrugged it off, but it wouldn't be the last time that I'd hear "war criminal."

That same afternoon, a new and much more physical form of harassment began that was to continue for the rest of my time in solitary. They ran the heat up to what must have been 130 degrees and left it there for an hour and a half or so – a prolonged sauna. I stripped to my shorts and lay as still as I could on my bunk. I would soon soak the already filthy mattress with sweat. The fleas, apparently activated and agitated by the heat, raced frantically back and forth over my exposed skin and chewed on me as if in retribution. Swatting at them was futile and only served to increase my body heat. By the time they turned the heat back down I was totally exhausted, both physically and mentally, and covered with fleabites. The guard brought my evening meal – a piece of black bread and a cup of barley soup.

As I lay on my bunk that night, I assessed my situation. In just the short time I'd been here, the harsh conditions, the inadequate nourishment, the threats, the heat treatments, and the swarms of fleas were beginning to take a toll. I had no idea how long they would keep me here, but in order to survive, I knew I had to do something to keep my mind and body fit. By the morning of that third day, I had developed a survival plan – it consisted simply of daily physical and mental exercise. I would start with fifteen minutes of calisthenics every morning followed by fifteen minutes of reciting aloud from any stories, speeches, poems, and prayers that I could remember. I would repeat this routine every hour throughout the day. I also decided that I would, to the extent possible, go on the offensive. I would try to figure out ways to hassle the guards. I put my plan into action that third day and pretty well stuck to it throughout my stay in solitary.

So I settled into a routine of sorts: Get up, toilet call, physical exercise, mental drills, black bread washed down with bad coffee, plan of the day to pester the guards, more exercises, noon coffee, exercises, afternoon "sauna," complete exhaustion, black bread and gruel, try to sleep. Most of the time when I wasn't engaged in my exercises, I let my mind drift back and forth between the past and the present. I tried not to contemplate the future. I was determined to make it through each day as it came.

My mother and father were both raised on farms in northern Illinois. Like most rural families in the early 1900s, they attended small country schools, often one room for the whole school, and learned and assimilated basic country values: Hard work, honesty, love of God and country, and strong family ties. My father went to veterinary school and practiced veterinary medicine for some years. Some time before I was born he switched and became an area distributor for the Chandler Auto Company but was always referred to by the local folks as "Doc Achen." The family was living in Kenosha, Wisconsin, a mid-sized manufacturing town near the Illinois border. When I was born in July, 1921, I was the third son. My brothers, Bob and George, were then four and six, respectively.

By the early 1920s my father had become moderately successful in his business and the family was financially sound. But my mother and father never lost their love of the country and believed that their sons should be raised on a farm. So in 1925, when I was four, the family bought and moved to a sixty-acre farm outside of Kenosha. My father kept and worked at his business, which continued to prosper. My mother took care of the household. Most of our land was leased to and farmed by a neighbor. We fenced the front ten acres where we raised a vegetable garden and kept two milk cows, three ponies and a hundred or more chickens. We had a hired hand, Frank, who tended to the outside chores, and a nanny, "Nana," who looked after us kids and helped with the household chores. When I was five we acquired Petsy, a German shepherd that was a daughter of Rin Tin Tin, the famous movie dog. She followed me around during the day and guarded the house at night. My brothers were in school most days and, being so much younger, I was seldom part of their activities when they were home. They avoided me as much as they could. They always seemed to be running away from me and I was trying to keep up, thus I learned to run. We had no near neighbors, so Petsy became my companion and best friend. I learned how to get along on my own in those formative years.

That is not to say we weren't close as a family. Often on the weekends when my father wasn't working we would go on picnics and other family outings. Mother read to us at night and helped my brothers, and later me, with our homework. Father taught us to ride the ponies and how to handle guns. I got my first shotgun, a single-barrel twenty gauge, when I was eight. We often hunted together and it was a strict rule that we didn't shoot anything we couldn't eat nor did we shoot any game bird that wasn't on the wing. Together our parents instilled in us the values which they had learned growing up and, though not demonstrative, set a loving and caring example for us.

One day, when I was nine years old, as I got home from school, I heard Frank, our hired hand, yelling, "Help! Help!" I ran to the barn where he was standing pointing at the door that housed the family vehicle. I opened the door and saw that my father was lying unconscious with his leg caught on the front bumper of the car. The engine was running and the room was filled with fumes. Frank didn't know how to shut the engine off and hadn't been able to get my father free of the bumper. Fortunately, I had watched my father, and knew how to kill the engine. We were then able to untangle my father's leg and drag him outside. In a few minutes, he started coming around and within an hour or so was fully recovered. Several days later, he asked me to take a walk with him. We walked in silence for ten or fifteen minutes. Then he sat me down on a log and sat beside me. He said, "Your mother tells me you saved my life." I didn't know what to say, so I said nothing. He put his arms around me and said, "Thank you, Son." I will never forget that moment of intimacy. It was the first and would be the last time my father ever hugged me. Six months later, he died from a brain tumor.

My first attempt to harass my captors got a strong reaction – almost too strong. I sat against the door so when the guard opened the peephole to check on me, he couldn't see me. He slammed the peephole and started shouting. Another guard came running and, after a short conversation, he looked through the peephole. Now the conversation became frantic and I was sure that they thought that if I'd somehow managed to escape, they were in big trouble. They jerked the big door open and almost stumbled over me as they entered with guns drawn. One started kicking me and both were screaming. I couldn't understand what they were saying, but it was clear they were not happy. A little later another guard, who spoke passable English, came and lectured me severely. Objective accomplished!

The food continued to be both awful and inadequate. From the little I remembered of our lectures on the Geneva Accords, POWs were supposed to get roughly the same fare as their captors. I didn't believe for a minute that the Germans were eating the garbage I was getting. One day I told the guard that where I came from stray dogs ate better. Either he didn't understand my limited German accompanied by hand signals or else he wasn't impressed. He just shrugged and took my tray.

Harassment plan number two backfired a little bit. I think it was the evening of the fourth day just after I'd railed at the guard about the bad food. As he was picking up my tray from what passed as the evening meal, I very carefully explained to him, again with charade style signals, that for breakfast I wanted eggs, Black Forest ham, white bread toast, and orange juice. At first he seemed a bit puzzled as I imitated a chicken (puck, puck, puck), and a pig (snort, snort), but he kept nodding and saying, "Ja, ja," like he understood. I chuckled for some time after he left, picturing how he was going to try to explain my demands to his superiors.

The next morning he brought my breakfast on a small tray covered with a cloth napkin and announced that he had brought my ham and eggs as requested. Two other guards stood watching in the doorway as I uncovered my breakfast – black bread and ersatz coffee! The guards all roared. This one was on me.

I searched my mind for poems and speeches that I'd been required to memorize as a student. I could pretty well recite the Gettysburg Address and Shakespeare's "All the World's a Stage" speech from "As You Like It." I also remembered most of William Cullen Bryant's "So Live" from "Thanatopsis" and, my all-time favorite, "The Shooting of Dan McGrew" by Robert W. Service.

The first time I tried the Gettysburg Address, I was sitting on my bunk reciting softly, struggling to remember the exact lines, when I heard the peephole door open. I continued reciting and, though I didn't look toward the door, I knew the guard kept watching until I finished and then quietly closed the peephole. I thought about this for a while and decided that the next time I recited, I'd stand up on the bunk and act it out – see what kind of reaction I could get. Maybe they would put me in a padded cell.

65

My life changed pretty dramatically in the early 1930s. My father had died, my brothers were away at different boarding schools and, though I didn't fully understand the "Great Depression" that my teachers talked about, I knew that our family economics had changed. The income from my father's business was gone so my mother and I had to make do. Nana had left us to get married and Frank had to seek work elsewhere because we couldn't afford to keep him on. I milked the cows, fed the chickens and gathered eggs, brought in the firewood, and did other chores as needed. One day my mother told me to take the two cows down to the neighbor's to get them "serviced." It was quite an enlightening experience for a ten year old boy who had never even been told about the birds and the bees. To this day, when asked if I want my car serviced, I say, "No, thank you. Just grease it and change the oil."

I also took music lessons, piano and drums, not of my own volition. Scarce as money was, my mother felt that I needed to learn something besides farming. We still had a pony, Prince, which I cared for and rode when I had time. Petsy, our shepherd, had a litter and we kept a male we named Bing. Petsy and Bing guarded the place well, which was important in those days. The farm was located near the crossroads of Highways 41 and 50, which connected Chicago and Milwaukee. We were told that many of the Chicago gangsters, including Al Capone, used to pass by on their way to hideouts near Lake Geneva in Wisconsin. This may or may not have been true, but what we did know was that the tough times brought a lot of hitchhikers and hobos along the highway. Many stopped by the farm, offering to work for food. Seldom did my mother find work for them, but she always gave them food. I learned a lot about farming in those years, at least enough to know that I didn't want to make it my life's work.

In 1934, my mother rented the two upstairs bedrooms to boarders. She let one room to Mr. and Mrs. Long and daughter, Francis, and the other room to Miss Ruby Bice. Both Mrs. Long and Miss Bice were schoolteachers. Francis was a freshman in high school, and Mr. Long worked at a store in town. Mother prepared breakfast and dinner for everyone and made box lunches to carry. Everybody got along well. My mother also found a fiddler, Mr. Alstead, and the three of us, mother on the piano, Mr. Alstead on the fiddle, and me on the drums, took in a little extra money playing Saturday night dances around the community. Sometimes Francis joined us and she and I sang. I don't know how much money my mother and Mr. Alstead made, but I got a whole dollar. My singing career came to an end one day when my mother told me that my voice was changing and I sounded like a forlorn yodeler. At about that same time, I was doing the dishes with Francis one night and looking at her when a new and unfamiliar feeling came over me. I was in love! Some weeks later, at the end of the school year, the Longs moved away and I was devastated. I rode Prince to the far end of the farm, sat on a rock and cried. My first time in love and my first love lost. Both would happen again in my young life.

On the fifth or sixth day in solitary, I stood on my bunk and, with great enthusiasm, including gestures, I began reciting the Gettysburg Address. "Four score and seven years ago, our Fathers brought forth... " Along about, "We have come to dedicate a portion of that battlefield as a final resting place... ", I heard the peephole open. I turned up the volume and punched the air vigorously. "But we cannot dedicate, we cannot consecrate, we cannot hallow this ground... " and a rousing finish, "and for the people shall not perish from the earth." All in all, I thought it was a stirring performance but I wasn't sure how the "audience" received it. The next morning I got an indication.

From my perch on the bunk, I recited, and this time with real personal feeling, "... So live that when thy summons comes to join the innumerable caravan in the silent halls of death, go not like the quarry slave scourged to the dungeon. But, sustained and soothed by an unfaltering trust, wrap thy drapery of thy couch about thee and lie down to pleasant dreams." Somewhat choked up at the impact of these prophetic words, I sang "God Bless America." My attempt to tease the guards only made me melancholy. But when, at the end of my heartfelt rendition, the guard opened the door and, with a big grin, said in his broken English, "God isn't going to like that singing," I had to laugh. When the guard had closed the door and was gone, I recited, this time to myself, "All the world's a stage and all the men and women merely players..."

VIII

INTERROGATION

I guess I'd been in solitary confinement for nine or ten days. The fleas that infested the cell seemed to be getting bigger and meaner every day. The more I swatted them, the more they chewed on me. Just to pass the time I had tried keeping track of "confirmed kills," but had given up when the count reached triple digits. They finally sent for me shortly after noon that day. I had just eaten an "improved" lunch, which meant I hadn't gagged, when one of the regular guards opened my cell door. Beside him was a German soldier I had never seen before. The unfamiliar soldier said in passable English, "Come with me." I suspect my heart rate went up by about fifty beats per minute. I sensed that my time had come, but for what I wasn't sure. I didn't know if they were going to question me, torture me, or shoot me. I was frightened beyond words, but I was determined not to show it to my captors. I asked my escort if I could stop at the latrine on the way. He nodded assent.

Alone in the latrine, I washed my hands and face with cold water. Then it struck me that I'd better urinate so that my bladder would be empty – just in case. I leaned against the wall and took as many deep breaths as I could, hoping to clear my head and prepare myself for whatever lay ahead. Finally, when I figured I couldn't stall any longer, I raised my eyes and said, "Okay, Lord, it's you and me." When we walked out of the building into the courtyard, I looked at the sky that I had not seen in many days and I felt a calmness come over me. I was ready.

We walked along a dirt road for a hundred yards or so, entered an office-type building and stopped at a door simply numbered 47. The guard knocked and there was a response in German. The guard opened the door, motioned me in and left. A man in a German uniform without rank or insignia was seated behind a large wooden desk. He had dark hair combed straight back, a neatly trimmed mustache, and piercing brown eyes. He looked to be no more than twenty-five to thirty years old. In a cultured voice with only a trace of an accent, he said, "My name is Hanns Scharff. Please come in and be seated. I am your interrogator." I was to learn later that Hanns Scharff, this disarmingly pleasant looking young man, was the "Master Interrogator" for the Luftwaffe.

The room was sparsely appointed with the one desk, two chairs, and a small table with several binders on it. The desk was clear except for an ashtray and a large blue three-hole binder lying to the side. On the wall behind the desk were two enlarged photographs of men in uniform. When I glanced at them, I was startled to see that one was Colonel Blakeslee, Commander of the 4th Fighter Group. I didn't immediately recognize the other one, but later learned it was Captain Don Gentile, a renowned ace and the first fighter pilot to surpass Eddie Rickenbacker's record of thirty-six victories in World War I. Seeing the photos, I had quickly looked away so as not to show any sign of recognition.

The interrogator asked me if I would like a cigarette. I would have loved one, but since I had not had a cigarette for over two weeks, I was afraid it would make my head spin and I knew I needed all the wits I could muster. I said, "No, thank you." He nodded and said something in German. When I didn't respond he stared at me for a long time and then said in English, "You speak German, don't you?"

I said, "My name is Norman Achen, Lieutenant, 0756430."

"Do you know you have relatives here in Germany living along the Rhine River?"

I didn't know if that was true or not but wondered, if it was true, how in the hell did he know that?

I responded with my name, rank, and serial number.

"Why are you here fighting against the Fatherland?"

Herr Scharff displayed no impatience or anger at my refusal to answer. Between questions, he kept his eyes locked on mine and, determined not to show weakness, I returned his gaze.

Without taking his eyes off me he pointed over his shoulder at the photographs and said, "Do you know who these men are?"

I responded with my name, rank, and serial number.

"If you are who you say you are, you know them. They haven't been in to see me yet, but they will. I keep their pictures here so that I will immediately recognize them when they arrive." He said this in a taunting manner, and I knew it was meant to rattle me.

He said, "You claim you are Lieutenant Achen. How do I know you are not lying? How do I know you are not a spy?"

I repeated my name, rank, and serial number, but the question puzzled me. I had been searched several times, including a full stripped-down body, when I entered the Frankfurt interrogation center. Early on they had taken my dog tags, which had my name, rank, and serial number, and I had never been out of custody since. How could they not know who I was? Scharff kept staring at me. I finally said, "You have my dog tags."

Scharff snapped back, "I have dog tags that say I'm General Eisenhower. Does that make me General Eisenhower? The name Achen is German. Do you have relatives in Germany?" As he asked this, he abruptly got up and turned as if to leave the room.

I responded with my name, rank, and serial number, but this time I changed two of the numbers to see if he would catch it. He turned back and looked at me. Just a trace of a smile crossed his face. He'd caught it.

Scharff left the room. I assumed I was being watched in some manner so I sat immobile, trying to look nonchalant. But my mind was racing. What was the interrogator driving at? Did they really have a doubt as to my identity? Did they think I was a spy? That I'd purposely crash-landed in order to get into the prison system to spy on them? It just didn't make any sense. I decided that if some questions were asked that had no military significance I would answer them. Maybe by doing so I could find out what Mr. Scharff was getting at.

I was alone for about five minutes. When Mr. Scharff returned, he had a small reel of film. He sat with the film in his right hand, absentmindedly rubbing it with his left thumb, all the while watching me closely. Without taking his eyes off mine, he reached over and moved the blue binder in front of him. He opened the binder to the first page, placed it in front of me and said, "Look at this, please."

The page was titled, in both German and English, "Eagle Squadron and 4th Fighter Group." He turned the page and there was an aerial photograph of the 4th Fighter Group base at Debden, England. He said, "In the past five years I have interrogated every pilot captured from the Eagle Squadron, now known as the 4th Fighter Group. The group has been stationed at Debden Airbase since 1940. Can you show me where your airplane was parked?"

I thought it over for a few moments and answered, "Yes." I pointed to my Mustang.

449.

9.	2nd Lt.	DAVIS	Mustang	K43 7451	USAAE	374	367
10.	Maj.	BARLOW	Typhoon	J 591	SAAF	182	124
11.	Cpt	LOWMAN	Thunderbolt		USAAE	365	358
15.	Maj	KELLER	Lightning	J 7970	"	434	479
17.	Cpt	CLARK	Thunderbolt J1847	"	82	118
17.	May	ELLEDGE	Thunderb.		"	506	404
1.	1st Lt.	Tiorle	Mustang		"	343	55
1.	2nd Lt.	DIFFENBAUGH	"	J 1877	'	383	364
25.	Maj	SMITH	"		'	334	4
16.	Cpt.	NURTZ	"		"	354	355
14.	2nd Lt.	SHAW	"		"	505	339
87.	Cpt	GODFREY	"	J 992	"	336	4
	2nd Lt.	ACHEN	"	J 7951	"	384	4
1.	"	PISKLAK	Thunderbolt J 1944	"	412	373
28.	"	CHERRY	Mustang J 995	"	368	357
1.	1st Lt.	BURKHARD					

Sept.

1.	Cpt.	RYAN	Thunderbolt J	"	410	373
2.	1st Lt.	DOERING	Mustang J	"	77	20
4.	Col.	WILSON				20
5.	Lt. Col.	GABRESKI	Thunderbolt			56
6.	1st Lt.	MILLS	Lightning	"	429	474

He turned the page and continued, "Here is a list of the pilots in the the 4th Fighter Group."

I glanced at the page, which was indeed a list of names, many of which I recognized from the group. I said nothing.

Mr. Scharff turned another page and said, "I would like to show you an article from the Phoenix, Arizona, paper, dated October 2, 1943."

Again, I glanced at the page, but this time I did a double take. What I saw almost made me sick. It was a story about the graduating class for advanced pilot training at Luke Air Force Base, with the names of the graduates – my name included. I sat in stunned silence.

He said, "I have one more question to establish your identity. What wing is the 4th Fighter Group in?"

71

I did not know the answer to that question and I told him so. He tapped his fingers on the desk and stared at me for a long time. I kept my eyes steady, still wondering where this was going.

Finally, he asked, "Do you know why you have been kept in solitary confinement for the past ten days?"

I shook my head and said, "I have no idea."

Again, a long pause, studying me closely... and then very deliberately, emphasizing each word, "You have been accused of strafing and killing civilians," he leaned forward, "and if we prove it we will have to shoot you!"

I continued to stare at my interrogator but his face went out of focus and my stomach did a couple of flips. I opened my mouth to reply, but thought better of it. At best, I think that at that point anything I'd tried to say would have come out as a squeak or a gurgle.

After another long pause, letting his words sink in, "We have the film from the camera in your airplane. It was sent to Berlin to be developed and has just been returned." In saying this he held the film up as if this was the evidence that was going to convict me. "Can you tell me what is on this film?"

Now, I took a long pause – first, to get my emotions settled and, secondly, to decide how I was going to answer. I sensed that name, rank, and serial number was going to get me shot. I knew that if it was truly the film from my Mustang it was blank, but if I told him how I knew that, would I be disclosing an important military secret? And what if it wasn't my film? There could be anything on it and I'd be the loser. After thinking about it for a while, I concluded that they probably knew the answer and that, at any rate, it wouldn't be important information. The Germans had downed and examined hundreds... no thousands of our aircraft, including a fair number of P-51s.

Finally, I said, "Yes."

The Interrogator shot back, "How?"

I said, "If that film is really from my airplane, it is blank – there is nothing on it. I did not fire my guns the day I was shot down."

Mr. Scharff began tapping on the desk again, a slight frown as if thinking. Then, "You mean to tell me that you can't fire your guns without the cameras running?"

I said, "No, the camera will not turn on unless the guns are fired. The pilot has no control over this."

He did not respond to that, but picked up the phone and said something in German. After a few moments, Mr. Scharff spoke again and this time I heard him say, "Major Smith."

Several minutes passed. Mr. Scharff continued to tap on the desk. Then, "Snuffy, this is Hanns Scharff. Is it true that the guns on a P-51 cannot be fired without the camera running?" I couldn't hear the answer, but Mr. Scharff nodded and said, "You're quite sure?" He nodded again and turned to me, "Do you know Major Snuffy Smith?"

I knew Major Smith. He had been the operations officer for the 4th Fighter Group. I had flown missions and participated in several dogfights with him. I knew that he had recently been shot down and taken prisoner, but I doubted that he was really on the phone here. I believed that I was being set up.

My answer was guarded, "Maybe."

He said into the phone, "Lieutenant Achen is here with me. He would like to say hello and thank you. As he handed me the phone, I detected a slight smile and a twinkle in his eyes. He seemed relaxed. I thought, hoped, that maybe this really was Major Smith and, if so, maybe I was out of the woods.

When I took the phone and said, "Hello," the deep Texas drawl from the other end immediately convinced me that I was indeed talking to Major Snuffy Smith. I was so relieved that I hardly remembered anything that was said. I just knew that another Texan had saved my bacon just as Johnnie Godbolt had that night in Santa Ana. I lifted my eyes and said a little "Thanks" to the Texans.

Major Smith asked me about my wellbeing, and I inquired about his. While we were on the phone, an orderly came in and laid a note on Mr. Scharff's desk. I saw him glance at the note and smile broadly. He took the phone from me and said, "Snuffy, we just got Johnny Godfrey." Godfrey was a well-known pilot from our group. He added, "We also have Captain L.C. Smith from the 4th Fighter Group here, so tonight we will have a dinner for you."

With that, the interrogation was over. Mr. Scharff called the guard in and gave him instructions to get me cleaned up and taken out of solitary confinement. As I was leaving, he asked me if I now wanted a cigarette.

I laughed and said, "More than one."

He threw me the pack from his pocket and said, "Keep them and I'll see you tonight."

IX

THE DINNER

I left Mr. Scharff and the interrogation room in the highest spirits since I made my unscheduled landing and became a guest of the Third Reich. Even so, the number of Allied pilots who were prisoners of war saddened me. I had known that we'd lost a great number of bomber and fighter pilots, many whom I had known and flown with, but now it became a lot more personal. On the other hand, I was off the hook and just talking to Major Smith, circumstances as they were, was uplifting. He seemed to be in good spirits and had said they were not being mistreated.

I thought that Mr. Scharff was putting me on about the dinner invitation so, wanting to fill the time with something other than fretting, regretting and what-iffing, I prevailed on the guard escorting me back to my cell to find me a book. He took me to a room where there were some thirty books in English. I picked out the fattest one without regard to the title, subject, or author, and was returned to my cell.

I lay down amongst the gaggle of fleas that co-habited with me and tried to digest what had happened here. I knew from the intelligence briefings that this was not routine for captured fighter pilots. Why me? If they found the film from my gun cameras they should have noted that none of my ammunition had been expended. Had someone reported my aircraft strafing civilians? If so, they were mistaken. I had no idea why I was accused of such a brutal act. The more I thought about the whole situation the less I understood it.

I picked up my book and tried to concentrate on reading, but it was sweaty hot, my head ached, and I was definitely losing ground in my continuing battle with the fleas. I was considering offensive options when the huge wooden door to my cell swung open and two German guards stepped in. They stared at me for a moment and one said something in

German to the other. The other guard nodded agreement and then to me in broken English, "Mistake. You filthy. Not you," and they closed the door. As far as I could tell, none of the fleas left with them. I lit the stub of one of my precious cigarettes hoping that the smoke might keep them at least temporarily at bay. Didn't work.

Several minutes had passed when the cell door opened again and one of the same guards motioned for me to follow him. Shortly I was again standing before door 47. I thought, "Uh oh." The guard's knock was answered by that same polite, "Please come in." As the door opened I could see Mr. Scharff behind his desk and another gentleman in a dark business suit sitting nearby.

Mr. Scharff looked at me and, obviously irritated, said, "You can't go to dinner like that!" Since there were no mirrors in my cell I could only suspect what I looked like, but I could smell and I knew for sure I wasn't any rose. Mr. Scharff spit out a stream of instructions to the guard and then said testily to me, "Go get cleaned up." He had not spoken that harshly during my entire interrogation – even when he said they were going to shoot me.

It had been fifteen days since I last showered, shaved, and brushed my teeth at Debden. Most days I had sweated profusely while doing turf battles for my bunk. One particularly hot day I got to thinking that, had I been home in Wisconsin, even the cows would have shunned me.

I was taken to a shower room where I undressed and stepped under a glorious stream of hot water. They even gave me soap! It takes a long time to wash away fifteen days of sweat and grime, especially when you're savoring it as I was. But the guard, already chastised and undoubtedly given a timetable by Mr. Scharff, became impatient and motioned for me to get out. He gave me a razor, which had obviously been in service for some time, and, with some difficulty, I mostly disposed of fifteen days of facial hair growth. I then brushed my teeth. The toothpaste was foul and the toothbrush, like the razor, had also seen better days, but I didn't mind. I combed my hair and put on a clean shirt. Wow!

Back at door 47, I again felt mixed emotions about seeing American pilots as prisoners of war. But when I stepped into the room and saw Major Snuffy Smith, L.C. Smith, Johnny Godfrey, and Col. Loucks, I was overwhelmed. I wanted to cry, but instead I laughed and said, "Imagine seeing you all here!" They all laughed with me. The only one I knew was Snuffy, but Johnny Godfrey wore his U.S. flight suit, and

Col. Loucks was in a South African flight suit and even before being introduced I knew who they were.

Besides the prisoners in the room there was Mr. Scharff; Oberstleutnant (Obstlt) Killinger, the Camp Kommandant; and the man I'd seen earlier in Scharff's office, who we suspected was a Gestapo intelligence officer. The room was filled with tobacco smoke and they were all seated around a short-wave radio. It took a few moments for me to realize that the broadcast was in English. It was a news broadcast from the BBC. I was handed a beer and a cigarette and I sat down and listened to the news with the others. I had not heard any news since that morning I took off from Debden. From the briefing that morning I knew that a huge invasion had been launched in southern France. But I didn't know whether it had been successful or not nor did I know anything else about the progress of the war. And now I was hearing the astonishing news that the Allies had occupied Paris and that France had a provisional government headed by General de Gaulle. The announcer went on about the great celebration that was going on in Paris and how the Allied soldiers were being welcomed like heroes with kisses and flowers. Though uncertain about my own future, I felt great joy for the French and great pride in being an American soldier and, for the first time since I became a prisoner, I did not feel alone.

When the news ended, Obstlt Killinger turned off the radio. One of the Americans declared, "We will be in Berlin by Christmas!" I don't remember who made this rash declaration but it sure sounded good to me. In my mind I sang "I'll be home for Christmas." Four months later, Christmas 1944, I would remember this and the next line, "But only in my dreams."

As my mind drifted back, the argument about the outcome of the war went on and, incredibly, it was not about if, but only when. Snuffy Smith was saying in his deep Texas drawl that it would be over by the first of the year. One of the Germans said, "Maybe by spring." Some friendly bets were made but, to my great satisfaction, no one was betting on a German victory.

After an hour or so of "partying" in room 47, Obstlt Killinger announced that it was time for dinner. We walked about a quarter-mile to the only single house in the compound, which I presumed to be the Kommandant's personal quarters. As we walked along I noticed that none of my fellow prisoners except L.C. Smith had any discernible injuries. L.C. had been severely burned. I didn't ask, but guessed it happened

76

when he was shot down. It was obvious that he was undergoing skin grafts to his face and hands. This made me feel that if we had to be prisoners, we were lucky to be in the hands of the Luftwaffe. I didn't believe from what we'd been briefed that the Gestapo or the SS dealt with prisoners humanely and certainly didn't provide medical care of this nature.

When we entered the house we found a buffet set up with two German ladies to serve us. The dinner and the conversation were casual, as if we were guests and not prisoners of war.

Mr. Scharff talked about his background and how he came to be an interrogator for the Luftwaffe. He was born and raised in East Prussia but, at the time war broke out in Europe, was living and working in South Africa. In 1939, married with children, he and his family had been in Germany on vacation. With war raging through Europe, his exit visa was revoked. Soon thereafter he was drafted into the Wehrmacht and, through a series of twists and turns, became an interrogator for the Luftwaffe.

After dinner and a nightcap, Mr. Scharff took us back to our cells. He gave me an extra pack of cigarettes, shook my hand and wished me good luck.

I never saw Hanns Scharff after that night, but heard quite a bit about him from other pilots whom he had interrogated. In 1978, he collaborated with award-winning author, Ray Toliver, to write a fascinating book aptly named "The Interrogator." The book chronicled his unique methods and successes in getting information from Allied prisoners of war. In recent years, I have become friends with Hanns' son, Chris Scharff, a retired successful businessman, who is as personable and engaging as his father. We've spent many nights discussing his father for whom we share a mutual respect and admiration.

The following day while being transferred to a transit camp, Johnny Godfrey and I had a chance to discuss the events of the prior day. We were both puzzled by the short duration of the interrogation (once I had been cleared of war crimes), the friendly manner of our captors, and the general easy atmosphere that prevailed throughout the evening. We concluded that the Germans knew that the end of the war was near and it couldn't hurt to have a few ex-POWs who might speak favorably of them at some later time, or maybe they just sensed that neither of us had any information of significance to them. Whatever the reason, it worked for us.

X

STALAG LUFT III

I lay on my bunk with my ever-present companions and reflected. The day I was shot down and taken prisoner was the most dreadful and terrifying day of my young life. The day I just went through was the most incredible. In the last twelve hours my range of emotions ran the whole spectrum: from apprehension when summoned by the guard, to firm resolve when I faced the interrogator, near panic when told I had been accused of war crimes and might be shot, and finally, cautious relief when I recognized Snuffy Smith's drawl and believed that I was going to be cleared.

And then, there was the evening: A casual and even congenial party and dinner with our Nazi captors, including a Gestapo agent, bets about when the Allied armies would enter Berlin, reminiscences of better days by the Germans, and then the hand shake and "Good luck" from the interrogator. Amazing!

Although I hadn't been challenged physically, the emotional drain was enormous. I felt like laughing then crying or screaming or beating on the wall, but I had no energy for any of that. As I lay there, arms and legs akimbo, I felt like a rag doll with fleas. Only my mind was moving. My thoughts alternated between the past and the future. I thought about some of the things that I used to think were tough, like the times back on the farm when I had to go out before daylight in freezing weather to milk the cows. At that time I thought that had to be the worst thing that could happen to me. Now, lying here in a German prison cell, alone, frightened for my family and about a future that seemed uncertain at best, those days became the good old days. Thinking about how I hated milking cows and, I suppose, in a release of nervous tension, I started laughing out loud. Immediately the peephole in the door opened up and

I knew the guard was watching me. That made me laugh even more. He must have thought I'd gone over the edge.

And what about the future? At dinner there had been no discussion about what was going to happen next. At Debden, we had been briefed on the "normal" chain of events when an American pilot was captured, but since I didn't think that would ever happen to me, I didn't pay much attention. From what I remembered, though, prisoners were interrogated at the Luftwaffe Interrogation Center near Frankfurt for three or four days and then sent on to one of several permanent prisoner of war camps known as Stalag Lufts. I didn't know how the advance of the Allies and the apparent impending defeat of the German armies would affect the treatment of POWs, but guessed I would soon find out.

The next morning, about a hundred of us were marched to the train station and loaded onto a train. After about an hour of riding on the train we arrived at the small town of Wetzler, about thirty miles northwest of Frankfurt. I knew where Wetzler was on the map because there were important optical factories there that made bombsights. I had escorted our bombers there on at least one occasion. We detrained and were marched to a guarded compound called Dulag Luft. It turned out that Dulag Luft was a transitional camp where POWs drew supplies and were assigned and sent to the permanent camps. We spent most of the day in lines, drawing personal gear, clothes shoes, toilet articles and such. Sometime in the mid-afternoon, we were assembled and prepared to march back to the train station where we were to board a train that we speculated would be taking us to our Stalag Luft, wherever that may be.

But just as we were waiting for the order to march, my name and Johnny Godfrey's name were called out and we were told to step out of the formation. As I made my way through the ranks my stomach tightened and I thought, "Oh, Lord, what now?"

As the others marched off, Johnny and I were led to a nearby building and told to sit down in what appeared to be a waiting room. We sat silently, assuming that we were being watched and/or listened to. After a fifteen or twenty minute wait, a German officer, a Colonel I believe, came out of the inner office and, in good English, told Johnny to come with him. I sat alone in the waiting room for some thirty minutes, still wondering why we had been singled out. When they came out, Johnny made an 'I don't know what's going on' face and shrugged. The Colonel beckoned me in to the office and politely asked me to sit. He introduced himself as Colonel, but I don't recall his name, and said he was from Military Intelligence. He offered me a beer and a cigarette. I accepted the cigarette but reluctantly declined the beer. When he spoke his tone was casual, inquisitive, but non-threatening.

"I have been told you lived in California. I have never been there but understand it is a very beautiful state." I nodded.

He continued, looking at a notebook in front of him. "I see that you took your flight training in Arizona and Florida, and that you came to England in late May, assigned to the famous Eagle Squadron, now part of the 4th Fighter Group, at Debden.

He looked up at me but I didn't respond. I was not surprised that he had this information, since Mr. Scharff knew when and where I had graduated from advanced flight training and that I flew with the 4th.

Still looking at me he said, "I understand you have close relatives here in Germany. Is that true?"

I said, "I am not aware of any relatives I may have in Germany."

He asked, "Why did you volunteer to enter the service?"

I replied, "I felt it was my duty to serve my country."

He said, "You have been flying your famed Mustang in combat for over two months now. Why is it that you have no victories?"

His tone and the implication of his question stung me. I shot back, "I believe that's the fault of the Luftwaffe since they couldn't put planes in the air – at least not on the days that I was flying."

Incredulously, "Are you telling me that you never ran into the Luftwaffe?"

"That is correct."

The Colonel frowned and shook his head. His tone became wistful. "Why did America enter the war against Germany after staying neutral for so long?"

I started to answer but he continued, "If the United States withdrew its forces now, we could still beat the Russians and then take on the English. Do the American people know that if you win this war you will sooner or later have to fight Russia?"

I had no knowledge of this issue so I simply shrugged my shoulders.

The Colonel stood and motioned towards the door. He said, "You and Captain Godfrey will be taken to the train now."

We were driven to the train station where we boarded a train with another group of POWS. We traveled all night and got off the train at

Sagan, Germany, early the next morning. We marched for several miles under the watchful eyes of a dozen or so guards with dogs. Around noon we arrived at Stalag Luft 3, our new "home" presumably until the end of the war. As we entered the compound gate, a crowd of several hundred POWs greeted us, looking for people they might know and hungry for information about the outside world and, particularly, how the war was going. There was a lot of handshaking and backslapping as old friendships were renewed and new friendships formed under these awful conditions of imprisonment in this foreign land.

Several people I knew greeted me and, when asked about the progress of the war, I stated with conviction that the German armies were reeling and that the Allies would be in Berlin by Christmas. I wasn't sure I really believed this but I thought that it wouldn't hurt to be optimistic. Some of these men had been prisoners for a long time – they needed good news.

While I was talking to some old friends, I saw out of the corner of my eye a huge blond man with a bad limp approach to my side. When I turned to him he stepped up and gave me a big hug. A bit startled, I stepped back.

He said, "I'm Aubrey Hewatt and I'm your roommate. C'mon, I'll introduce you to your other roommates."

Hewatt led me across the open area towards one of the barracks-type buildings on the northeast corner of the compound. He limped so badly that it took us nearly ten minutes to cover the hundred yards or so. As we walked along I took a good look at the barbed wire fences and the strategically placed guard towers with huge spotlights, each manned by two guards with a machine gun. I wondered if anyone had tried to escape and, if so, how they fared. It didn't look promising.

Also, as I looked around the compound at the barracks, the outside latrines, the fencing, and the towers, I thought about the Japanese-Americans at the camp I'd helped build at the Gila River Project. I wondered if they were also thinking about escaping from their "enemies."

We finally made it across the compound and into the barracks that was to be my home. The one-story building was divided into several large rooms. We entered a room where ten men awaited us. Hewatt introduced me around and each shook my hand warmly. The last man I was introduced to was the Room Commander, Harold Van Every. I didn't recognize him, but the name rang a bell somewhere off in my dulled senses. As he was welcoming me, I kept wondering why the name was familiar. And then it struck me.

He was still speaking as I blurted out, "You're from Minnesota, aren't you?"

He looked surprised and said, "Yes, do I know you?"

I laughed and said, "No, but I know you. You're Hal Van Every, the scat-back from the University of Minnesota!"

Now he laughed and said, "Well, I was a lot more scat then than I am now, but how did you know that?"

I told them the story. "You might remember that in '39 or '40, the University of Arizona played University of Minnesota at Minnesota. It was my understanding that U.A. believed that their football was at the stage of development where they could compete with the Big Ten teams such as Minnesota and they were anxious to prove it. A fraternity brother and good friend of mine, Eddie Held, played left end both defense and offense for U.A. The game was played on Saturday, but we didn't see Eddie until he came to dinner on Tuesday. Now, we'd seen Eddie after a lot of football games and he was usually pretty beat up. We'd all seen him play and he played hard. But this time he looked like he'd been through a meat grinder. Eyes were black, his nose and one ear were swollen, and he had bruises on most parts of his body that we could see We all knew what the game score was, but nobody mentioned it. Finally someone asked him to describe the Minnesota team.

Talking slowly, as though even talking hurt, he related, "I would see the scat-back get the ball and start around my end. I would get in my crouch-charge position and could see two pairs of legs about four feet apart leading the runner. I figured I could knife between the interference and nail the ball carrier. The problem was that when I tried to knife through, I found that these guys were running shoulder to shoulder. They were huge! And the one they called a "scat-back" weighed over two hundred pounds and ran like a deer. When I did get to him, he'd drag me ten yards before I could bring him down. I won't soon forget Hal Van Every and those thugs who ran interference for him."

"Every night at dinner for the next week or so we would ask Eddie to tell us some more stories about the Minnesota team and the now legendary scat-back. Each night the stories got better and you got bigger and faster. You probably remember that the final score was 62 to 0. The word around campus was that next time we challenged the University of Minnesota it'd better be at rodeo." Everyone had a good laugh.

In the next days and weeks life went from nightmare to bad dream to harsh reality as I settled into the routine of being a prisoner of war. It didn't take me long to realize that a unique type of relationship developed among the POWs. It was more than just friendship, it was like family and, in my case, having grown up more or less a loner, closer than family. Being with some twenty-five hundred English-speaking aviators in the same predicament as me may have been small comfort, but it was far better than the solitary confinement and the uncertainties that I'd been through. In a room with eleven other men, no locked doors and no fearful anticipation of interrogation, my outlook brightened considerably. I felt that I had endured the worst. I believed that the war would soon end in an Allied victory and that all I had to do now was hang on and everything would turn out okay.

My optimism was probably more self-indulgent than realistic, particularly the part about having endured the worst. It wasn't all roses. There were a lot of things not to like about being a prisoner of war and one consideration became paramount – hunger! Although I had been on scant rations in the twenty days it took me to get here and had lost some weight, I didn't ever remember being hungry. Several times during my period in solitary, I had wondered why a man who was about to be executed would want to order a last meal. I concluded that if it came to that with me, I would order several double martinis. But now that my living conditions were somewhat improved and I no longer feared immediately for my life, I very rapidly became hungry.

I was not alone. Hunger was a fact of life for all the POWs. The normal fare when I arrived at Stalag 3 was occasional ground horsemeat, some sauerkraut, blood sausage (mostly inedible, even to half-starved prisoners), black bread, ersatz jam, and some kind of unrecognizable vegetable. Each barracks had a small room with a cooking stove and a schedule was made up allotting each room a time to prepare their meals. Cooking duties within each room were rotated. Some were exempted from this duty because, as bad as the food was, they managed to make it worse.

In addition to the food supplied by the Germans, each prisoner received a weekly Red Cross package. These parcels generally contained a can each of tuna, spam, and corned beef, powdered or condensed milk, powdered coffee, a package of crackers, three packs of cigarettes, a package of raisins, a tin of butter, and a chocolate bar. The cigarettes and chocolate bars were excellent items to trade with the guards for favors or goods of one kind or another. The condensed milk was usually caramelized by boiling and mixed with ground crackers and raisins to make a very passable dessert. Before the Germans passed out the parcels, they punctured the canned goods to prevent them from being stored up for escape. This forced us to eat them pretty quickly. Someone had figured out how to partially seal the punctures with a drop of melted butter but this didn't prolong their life but a day or so.

Shortly after my arrival it was announced that prisoners would be going on half rations. This bad news almost caused a revolt but cooler heads prevailed and convinced the rest that an uprising would only lead to a lot of bloodshed – prisoner's blood – and achieve nothing. So life went on and hunger became more profound. One of our fellow prisoners, Lieutenant Larry Paelan said it well in a poem he sent to his wife:

> *"I dream as only captive men can dream*
> *Of life as lived in days that went before;*
> *Of scrambled eggs, and shortcakes thick with cream;*
> *And onion soup and lobster thermidor;*
> *Of roasted beef and chops and T-bone steaks*
> *Of sausage, maple syrup, buck wheat cakes,*
> *And chicken broiled or fried or a la king.*
> *I dwell on rolls or buns for days and days,*
> *Hot corn bread, biscuits, Philadelphia scrapple,*
> *Asparagus in cream or hollandaise,*
> *And deep-dish pies, mince, huckleberry, apple.*
> *I long for buttered, creamy oyster stew,*
> *And now and then, my pet, I long for you."*

Stalag Luft 3 was a huge prison complex divided into five contiguous but separate compounds designated Compound East, West, Central, North, and South. I was in Compound West. Each compound housed some two thousand prisoners and was surrounded by two ten-foot barbed wire fences six feet apart with several rolls of concertina in between. There was a guard tower on each corner. About thirty feet inside the inner fence, and about two feet above the ground was a single strand of electrified wire encircling the compound. I was told that anyone who stepped over that wire would be shot from the tower. The entire complex of Stalag 3 was run by the Luftwaffe and was exclusively for captured Allied aviators. Our senior officers were constantly concerned that the prison would be taken over by the SS, who ran most of the POW camps. We all knew from numerous sources that Allied aviators were treated better than the other POWs. Goering himself, who wanted to protect the German pilots captured by the Allies, mandated the better treatment. None of us were big fans of Hermann Goering, but I must admit we were thankful for his "benevolence."

There were no formal courses or indoctrination programs on how to live as a prisoner of war. You had to watch, listen, and learn by trial and error. Some had been here for several years and some, such as me, for only a few days. The older prisoners, that is the ones who had been there longer, generally tried to help and tutor the new guys on how to survive and get along with the least amount of trouble. Although we all lived under the same conditions, prison life affected people in varied ways. Most of us tried to stay active, believing that was the best way to keep our minds and bodies healthy. But some simply lay in their bunks all day waiting for the war to end. A few seemed to have gone over the edge. Some would babble; some just sit and stare at something or someone far-off that the rest of us couldn't see. One man walked around all day with a toothbrush in his mouth, afraid that he was going to lose his teeth. Another circled the compound endlessly, carrying his Bible. Sometimes I wondered if I shouldn't be doing the same thing.

There were two formations each day, one in the morning and one in the evening. The purpose of the formations was to count heads to make sure no one had escaped. The formations were held on the exercise field where we would line up and be counted by barracks. Every so often one or more of the prisoners would hide in the barracks. This would throw the count off and send the guards scurrying to find the missing men. The rest of us would have to stand in formation until the culprit, or culprits, were found or until the Germans decided that someone had actually escaped. Since no one had escaped, or even attempted to escape, during the time I was there, we were all pretty sure that it was just somebody playing mind games with our captors. Though it was satisfying to see the Germans jumping through hoops, it was not fun having to stand for prolonged periods in formation, particularly when it was cold and raining or snowing. When there was warning of an air raid, all lights were doused and, when the alert was over, we again had to stand formation and be counted.

Those who wanted to could keep themselves occupied. Some sports equipment made its way to us, mainly through the Salvation Army. We played baseball when weather permitted, and in December when the weather really got cold, we took a hose and made an ice rink for hockey. We had non-denominational church services every Sunday, presided over by different POWs who, if not real preachers, at least had knowledge of the Bible. Once a week we were allowed a two-minute hot shower – forty at a time would soap up and then rinse off. We played Contract Bridge a lot. Partnerships were formed and bidding strategies, probably never heard of before or since, developed.

Mealtime, except for the days we received our Red Cross parcels, was always a mixed blessing. We were all terribly hungry, but the food supplied by the Germans was meager and awful. Some days it would be so odious I would get the dry heaves just smelling and looking at it - dry heaves because there was nothing in my stomach. It affected most others the same way. One day we got so desperate that we caught a stray cat, which we cooked and tried to eat. It was so tough and tasted so bad that we gave up after a few bites. We were all sorry we'd killed the cat.

We spent a lot of time discussing the status of the war and how it affected us. Some enterprising prisoners had bribed guards to smuggle parts in and had eventually constructed a short-wave radio. It was kept hidden but the guards knew it existed and ignored it. Every day one of the inner circle would visit each barracks and report on the progress of the war. We speculated on how the Allied advances would affect our treatment by the Germans. Some thought that, because they were losing and suffering like us from lack of food, they would take it out on the prisoners. Others felt that they knew that defeat was imminent and would treat us well in order to get a better shake after the war.

These sessions would often bring on discussion about the Geneva Convention. Mostly it was the senior officers, who were more familiar with the Accords and what they meant, who carried the discussion. The younger of us did more listening. As trainees we heard the Geneva Convention mentioned quite often, but there was not a lot of emphasis placed on it. We were told that the Accords were international law on the treatment of the wounded and POWs and were led to believe that the nations which signed the treaty, including the USA, France, Britain, Germany and Italy - the major combatants of the war in Europe - would adhere to it. Furthermore, Geneva Convention aside, most of the prisoners involved in the discussions that I heard had believed that all combatant nations would treat POWs humanely. We mistakenly believed that "civilized" nations had basically the same values as the U.S. when it came to humane treatment of human beings. But early in the war we had heard the horror stories of Japanese atrocities, the most infamous being the "Bataan Death March." We had also heard stories of atrocities committed against Allied prisoners by the Germans, predominantly by the SS, the Gestapo and the Hitler Youth. Most disturbing were the stories of brutal treatment perpetrated by the Germans and the Russians against each other. It showed us what the Nazis were capable of, especially with the war going badly.

In fact, a major atrocity and violation of the Geneva Accords had been committed here at Stalag Luft 3 some months before I arrived. It involved a mass escape, later to be immortalized in a book and movie as "The Great Escape." From the discussions I heard, and it was discussed often, it was a well-planned escape that, through an unforeseen circumstance, went dreadfully wrong. The prisoners from the East Compound had, over a period of months, dug a long tunnel starting under one of the barracks and extending under the fences to a wooded area outside the compound. The escape began after the evening formation in order to give the escapees some twelve hours before the next formation and certain discovery by the Germans. The tunnel only provided crawl space, so the going was slow. Shortly after all of the hundred or so would-be escapees had entered the tunnel, disaster struck in the form of an air raid warning. As soon as the alert was over, a head count was taken and the men discovered missing. I didn't know the details of how many actually got through the tunnel, but all but two or three were recaptured within a day or two. On direct orders from Hitler, the first fifty caught were taken to remote locations and shot, one at a time. It was reported they had tried to escape. This was a clear violation of the Geneva Convention, but apparently effective. No one in any of the compounds of Stalag Luft 3 had attempted to escape since then.

XI

CHRISTMAS 1944 –
BATTLE OF THE BULGE

Sometime in August of 1944, American Brigadier General A. W. Vanaman was interned as a prisoner of war at Stalag 3. His story was that he had been an observer on a B-17 that was hit by flack somewhere over Germany. The pilot ordered everyone to bail out and he, not being a regular crew member and therefore unfamiliar with emergency procedures, was ordered to exit first. But a story was later circulated that after the General bailed, the pilot determined that the plane was flyable and they made it back to England.

Over time we all came to believe that the story was a set-up and that General Vanaman had volunteered to be captured so that he could influence the treatment of Allied prisoners. It turned out that he had been the military attaché at the American Embassy in Berlin, knew Field Marshall Goering personally and had even met with Hitler on occasion.

As the senior POW, he was by Allied doctrine the commander of all Allied prisoners. The Germans recognized this, provided him with a staff car, and allowed him to travel freely to all the prison camps and to Berlin as necessary. He became a highly effective and respected liaison between the Germans and the POWs and was generally credited with improving conditions in the prisons and the welfare of the prisoners. I often thought that I would like to meet this courageous man and thank him. Maybe in the next life.

Along toward the middle of December, in the stillness of the night, we started hearing explosions far off to the east. Word got around that the Russians were approaching the Oder River, forty miles from us. Our spirits soared. About the same time, we heard the first news over the BBC of a huge German offensive in the Ardennes Forest. This campaign, soon to be known as the Battle of the Bulge, was devastating. We had all hoped that the war would be over by Christmas and now we were hearing from the guards and generally confirmed by the BBC that the Allied forces were getting the living hell knocked out of them. Every day the guards would tell us of new advances and victories by the Wehrmacht. The news was not encouraging.

I cannot even begin to describe what emotional days the 24th and 25th of December were for the prisoners. But, even with the bad news, on that Christmas day in 1944, most of us there at Stalag 3 tried to put on a good face and celebrate the day. Back in October, I volunteered to become the permanent cook for our room and since then I had been hoarding a little bit of this and that each week so that we could have a "feast" at Christmas. I had also put all the prunes I could get my hands on, along with some liquid, some sugar, and a bit of yeast into a large glass jar to ferment. I kept the hoarded food and the fermenting prunes hidden in the back of a cupboard. The guards were pretty casual then, so they didn't check and I got away with it.

So on Christmas day we feasted on hoarded food and drank what passed as "prune liquor." It was not a menu I suspected anyone would attempt to repeat over the years, but it worked for us that day. After dinner we all went to the community hall to see a Christmas play put on by some of the prisoners. Like the dinner, it wasn't Broadway, but it was entertaining and occupied our minds for a while. As we returned to the barracks, Christmas carols were being played over the loudspeakers. And just at lights out, they played "Lilly Marlane" followed by "I'll be home for Christmas." I'm not ashamed to say that I was sobbing by the time the last song was finished and, though the lights were out, I could tell I wasn't alone.

From late December of 1944 through January of 1945, living conditions for the prisoners of Stalag 3 deteriorated sharply. Red Cross parcels had been cut in half, and more cuts were expected. Many of us suspected that the German guards were taking the other parcels because their rations had been cut way back and they weren't faring much better than the prisoners. The Allies had achieved strategic air supremacy over the continent, which meant that they pretty much controlled daylight ground movement by trains and trucks. Towards the latter part of January we were hearing that Hitler's mighty offensive in the Ardennes was turning into a disaster for the German army. The siege on the U.S. 101st Airborne at Bastogne had been broken by Patton's 3rd Army and the Wehrmacht, mostly out of fuel, ammunition, and rations, was in disarray and barely hanging on. The booming of the Russian artillery was constant now and getting ever closer.

With the worsening military situation, the prison administrators were getting stricter and the guards becoming sullen and often abusive. Rumors were circulating that several of the guards had deserted, and that some were captured and shot. None of these rumors were confirmed but, under the prevailing conditions, they were believable.

Memories of the "Great Escape" and the fifty brave souls who were executed was on everyone's mind, especially those of us who were still looking for our own chance to escape. Another event in January had a mixed effect on the prisoners, further demoralizing some and strengthening the resolve of others to get out and away.

A group of about one hundred Allied airmen were moved into Stalag 3 from the infamous Buchenwald concentration camp. These were all airmen who had gone down over France and were recovered by the French underground. The Gestapo discovered the Allied airmen, captured them, and interned them all at Fresnes Prison in Paris. The members of the French underground captured with them were summarily executed by firing squad. Over the next several days, the Gestapo rounded up a number of French men and women accused or suspected of working with the underground and shot them. The Allied prisoners were taken to Buchenwald and interned under the jurisdiction of the SS. When they arrived at Stalag 3, it was immediately apparent that they had been terribly mistreated. It was obvious from seeing them and hearing their horrible stories that neither the Gestapo nor the SS were even paying lip service to the Geneva Accords. It had a chilling effect on all of us, particularly with the Russians getting closer and rumors that SS guards were coming to move us out so we couldn't be liberated by the Russians.

January 27, 1945

It was 8 p.m. and very cold, maybe ten degrees outside, when the ten thousand prisoners of Stalag 3 got word over the loudspeakers to be ready to move out in one hour. At first we thought it was a drill or some sadistic joke being played by the guards, but the message was repeated several times and the messenger, sounding deadly serious, added that anyone not in formation and ready to move by 9 p.m. would be severely punished. By the appointed time, it appeared that all the prisoners of

Stalag 3 West were in formation standing in the snow waiting to move. I assumed that the prisoners of the other sections were in a similar posture. After an hour or so, we were moved back into the barracks to wait for additional guards to arrive. Finally at around midnight we were moved out onto the road and started marching. By then the temperature had dropped a few more degrees. I figured that if I put on all of the clothes I possessed, I would be dressed for maybe 30 degrees – except for my shoes, which weren't suited for any type of cold weather and certainly not for marching in the snow.

There was a lot of confusion among the guards. Apparently there had not been much thought put into this operation. From the actions of our captors, the fragmented orders, rescinded orders and then counter-orders, we gathered that the extent of the planning was to get us out of there fast and begin marching south and out of reach of the advancing Russian army. Each prisoner was given a Red Cross parcel as we departed the camp but the only means we had to carry anything was the one blanket we each had. We rolled what items we could in our blanket and wrapped it around our neck and shoulders for warmth. If we tried to put too much in, the weight and the awkwardness was forbidding. So, precious as food was, much was discarded along the way. I kept the items I figured would keep me alive: two canned meats, the bread, prunes, candy bar, and all three packs of cigarettes, the most valuable of trading items. The rest I reluctantly tossed.

We marched from midnight until noon the next day and covered, I was told, close to twenty miles. It started snowing around 4 a.m. and continued most of the day. The prisoners from each compound marched in separate formations and, since we left in the dark and amid a lot of confusion, I don't know where our section was in relation to the others, but I wasn't aware of ever seeing any of the other groups during the entire march. We walked three or four abreast in a fairly tight formation, mostly to try to keep warm. Our column of some twenty-three hundred stretched for about three-quarters of a mile, but even in daylight with the visibility limited by the weather, I could only see for a couple of hundred yards in either direction. In that distance I could see maybe half a dozen guards, some with dogs, so I figured that at most there was only thirty or so for the entire section. We were given a fifteen-minute rest stop every two hours. Most of us would sit and rub our feet to try to get some circulation going, but we couldn't sit long for fear of freezing.

Some of the men began to drop out of the formation shortly after the march began. These were the prisoners who were so weak from malnutrition, disease, or injuries that they couldn't walk for any distance at all. Some would be helped up by their buddies and with help go on for a ways before they dropped again. Others would refuse help and just lie by the wayside. We later learned that almost all of those who dropped out were picked up either by a follow up group of German soldiers, or German farmers, and taken to barns or some type of shelter. Those who survived were later rounded up and taken back in to custody.

Along about noon on the 28th we came to a fair-sized town. I never did find out the name of the town, but it had a jail that would accommodate about five hundred bodies standing up and packed together. After some discussion among the guards and the senior American prisoner, it was decided that they would put the maximum five hundred men at a time inside to warm up. The warming period was one hour. I ended up in the last group, so my waiting period was four hours. During that waiting period we had to keep moving, mostly walking around in circles, to keep from literally freezing to death. By the time I made it inside I was so cold and tired that I almost didn't give a damn about anything. But once inside I savored the warmth, if not the odor, of my fellow prisoners and gave myself a motivational speech, "I will not go gentle." Somehow, in the standing room only, I managed to take all my clothes off and put the few dry things I had next to my body. I put the wet clothes back on over the top so now I was wearing every bit of clothing that I had.

When my group came out of the jail, it was about 5 p.m. and we were immediately put in formation and began marching. Again we marched through the night and until late morning when we reached the town of Muskau, close to thirty miles from where we'd begun the evening before. We were told that sometime in the night the temperature had dropped to ten degrees below zero. Of the twenty-three hundred POWs who left Stalag 3, fifteen hundred made it to Muskau. When the rest stops were made during that second night, a number of the prisoners would sit down on their blankets and go to sleep. It was nearly impossible to wake them and get them moving again. A few threw their packs down and ran off into the fields. If the guards saw them go, they made little or no attempt to stop them. There was no place to go – escape was easy at this point – chances of staying free and surviving were remote at best.

The guards had acquired a horse and wagon for their packs. The horse looked to be very old and had a lot of ribs sticking out. On the second night he dropped dead, so the guards discarded a lot of things that they were carrying and shouldered their packs. Several times I saw guards carrying their dogs because the dogs' feet were frozen and they couldn't walk anymore. It made me wonder – they'd leave a man lying in the snow, mostly because they had to, but under these God-awful conditions would carry their dogs.

In the early dawn that second morning, through the light misting snow, I saw buildings off in the distance. Beautiful buildings! A place to stop and rest, get warm, maybe lie down and sleep. But as we got closer, the beautiful buildings turned out to be trees - a wooded area in the middle of nowhere. Not only was I greatly disappointed, I was shaken. Was I going over the edge?

From the time we left Stalag 3 in Sagan at midnight on the 27th of January until we arrived at Muskau on the 29th, we had marched nearly sixty miles. The Germans had not been able to provide us with any food and whatever we'd been able to carry of the Red Cross parcels was long gone. During that time I could only recall eating a box of prunes and a candy bar. I thought I'd started out with some other items so either I had eaten them, lost them at a stop, or tossed them along the way. I couldn't remember which. At a rest stop sometime that second day, some Polish slave laborers working at a nearby factory brought us hot water and one bottle of beer that three of us shared.

When we reached Muskau, which is an industrial city near Spremburg, we were broken down into groups and marched off to seek shelter. The group of about three hundred that I was in found shelter in a brick factory. We were all able to lie down on a huge sand floor above the furnaces. I was asleep by the time I hit the warm sand.

We stayed in the brick factory through the night of the 30th. One man who looked like he was near death was taken away. Another man went over the edge and started screaming and throwing anything he could get his hands on. He was finally restrained by the guards and also taken away. No food was provided.

Around noon on the 31st we were given a large slice of black bread and a small cup of barley soup. Shortly after that we were assembled, married up with the other groups, and marched off towards what I judged to be the south. I was told we were heading for Spremburg. I felt a lot stronger after the two day rest and, although our clothing had dried out, it was still awfully cold and, despite the "feast" of bread and soup, we were still weak from starvation. About two hours into the march it began to rain. Now we were not only cold and hungry, we were wet.

Just before dark we were told to find our own shelter and to assemble and be ready to move on the next day. Five of us got together and took off in the fading light to see if we could find a barn or shed to spend the night. It was still raining steadily and the roads were now crowded with refugees trying to get away from the advancing Russian army. After about an hour, we found a farmer who was willing to let us sleep in his barn. In exchange for some cigarettes, we had along the way acquired some bread and about a pound of cheese. The farmer's wife brought us a fair-sized pot of hot potato soup and we felt like we had died and gone to heaven.

About nine o'clock the next morning, word reached us that we were to assemble on the road and continue on to Spremburg, about four miles to the south. The refugees, many with horses or mules, some with wagons, and carrying all the possessions they could manage, were jamming the roads. Some of the guards went ahead moving them off the road so we could pass, but it still took us the better part of four hours to march the four miles to Spremburg.

At Spremburg, we were all put in an enormous tank repair building. For the first time since we left Stalag 3, our arrival had been anticipated and planned for. Huge iron cauldrons of hot barley soup awaited us and we were able to eat all we wanted. A high-ranking German officer addressed us over a loudspeaker. In very good English he told us that he had lived for a time in New York City. He said he regretted the hardships that we'd had to endure, but that it will give us strength for the even more difficult times that lay ahead. This was not something we particularly wanted to hear. He went on to say that the Russian army had crossed the Oder River and that civilization, as we knew it, would now perish. I assumed that by "we" he meant the Germans and I hoped that he was right. As he left, he "wished us well."

XII

40 OR 8 BOXCARS

At Spremburg we learned that about half of the prisoners from Stalag 3 had already passed through and were on their way to Stalag 7A at Moosburg, near Munich. We, on the other hand, were to be moved by train to Stalag 13D in Nuremberg.

It had been apparent and much discussed among the POWs for some time that the treatment of prisoners, at least in our Stalag, had become more callous and vindictive as time went on. We suspected that this was the case throughout the prison system. We knew that POWs in the Luftwaffe camps had been treated somewhat better than the general prison population, but that seemed to be changing. There was a lot of speculation as to why. It had started about the time of the "Great Escape." The decline of Marshall Goering's influence with the Fuhrer and that event were surely part of the reason, but most of us believed that the harsher treatment was also the result of a rising panic throughout Germany over the deterioration of the Third Reich's military situation. The fall of Paris, the ultimate disaster from the "Battle of the Bulge," the crossing of the Rhine, and finally, the inexorable advance of the dreaded Russian army, had turned the arrogance of early victories and the domination of Europe into desperation and despondency over the dawning inevitability of total humiliating defeat. The German Colonel at Spremburg had articulated what most Germans now realized when he said that "civilization, as we knew it, would now perish."

We heard that at this time in late January and early February of 1945, the Germans had more than one hundred thousand Allied POWs marching south and east trying to keep them away from the invading forces, To make matters worse, the Red Cross food parcels had stopped altogether. Then one of the strange paradoxes of war occurred.

The American High Command learned that the Swiss Red Cross was unable to deliver the food parcels and, knowing how desperate our situation was, somehow negotiated with the Germans an agreement to allow Allied trucks to deliver the parcels. So we waited at Spremburg, told only that food was on the way, and to our amazement and great joy, the parcels arrived. We didn't learn of the Allied involvement until later, but to fifteen hundred starving men, it was nothing less than a miracle. It turned out that there were four parcels for each five POWs, which created a dilemma of sorting and dividing. This was no small matter, but it was somehow accomplished without bloodshed as we prepared to march to the train station.

When we got to the marshalling yard, we were divided into groups to await boarding. While we were waiting, I spotted a German hospital train nearby. A fellow POW, known to me only as "Tex," and I went hunting for food. We found the kitchen car and traded two packs of cigarettes for eleven loaves of black bread. We weren't sure we had made such a good trade - American tobacco for German sawdust - but it was the best we could negotiate. When we returned to the station and distributed the bread among our group, we were hailed as heroes, at least temporarily, so our doubts about the trade went away.

Our train consisted entirely of boxcars, known to the Americans as "Forty or Eights," a name given to the smaller European boxcars by the American Horse Cavalry during World War I. It meant that you could get forty men or eight horses into them, The Germans apparently didn't consider this to be maximum capacity. Our boxcar ended up with fifty-three POWs and one guard. Just before the door was closed and locked from the outside, two guards hoisted a twenty-gallon wooden barrel into the car to be used as our only toilet facility. Even though we boarded around three p.m., the train didn't leave the station until near nightfall, after the Allied bombers and fighters had headed for home.

The next thirty-six hours were worse than anything we'd endured since we were marched out of Stalag Luft 3. With fifty-four men crammed into the boxcar, there was room for only about one-quarter of us to sit at any one time. Fortunately, Hal Van Every was in our group and he quickly took charge, dividing us into four groups to take turns sitting. So each group sat for an hour and stood for three. Every time the train swayed or jerked, which was almost constantly, those standing were thrown from side to side, against each other, the walls of the boxcar, and quite often on top of those who were sitting. But worse, with fifty-four unwashed bodies, many with diarrhea, one open barrel for toilet, and scant ventilation, the air quickly became so fouled that everyone started gagging. Those who didn't have a handkerchief found anything they could, including filthy socks, to put over their mouth and nose. These horrible conditions only got worse as time went by and more people got sick.

The train traveled very slowly and, being of low priority, was shunted onto sidings every few hours to let a train with higher priority pass. Sometime just after daylight the next morning, the train pulled into a station and we were allowed to get out for a few minutes and empty the toilet barrel. Some were so sick that they could barely crawl out of the boxcar. Many purged themselves right on the station platform.

After leaving the station we traveled for only an hour or two before the train pulled onto another siding, this time to sit all day in order to avoid the ever-increasing Allied air strikes against moving transport. Our boxcar door remained closed and locked all day.

By the evening when the train began to move again, the general condition of the prisoners had deteriorated to the point where only those who were too sick to stand were allowed to sit. The seated were placed in the middle so that the rest of us could take turns leaning against the boxcar walls. Progress was again terribly slow and the nearer we got to Nuremberg, the more often we were shunted onto sidings to wait while other trains passed.

One light moment occurred while we waited in one of the sidings. Our guard, who was not in much better shape than the POWs except that he sat the whole way, had dozed off with his rifle cradled loosely in his arms. One of the prisoners nearby gingerly lifted the weapon from him and it was passed along to the far side of the car. Moments later, the guard opened his eyes and realized that his weapon was missing. We expected a strong reaction, but he simply said, "Please give me my rifle." Someone said, "We didn't see any rifle. Are you sure you had one?" We all laughed and, since we had no use for one rifle in a locked boxcar, it was passed back to the guard. He took it without comment and went back to dozing.

The train pulled into the Nuremberg station about dawn and we exited the Hell Hole we'd been in and, with those of us who were able helping the ones too weak to walk on their own, marched to what would be our new Hell Hole – Stalag 13D.

Conditions at Stalag 13D were described very accurately in a U.S. Army intelligence report dated 1 November 1945, titled, "Stalag Luft 3" – It stated in part:

"Conditions at Stalag 13D were deplorable. The barracks, originally built to house delegates to the Nazi Party gatherings at the shrine city, had recently been inhabited by Italian POWs, who left them filthy. There was no room to exercise, no supplies, nothing to eat out of and practically nothing to eat insomuch as no Red Cross food parcels were available upon the Americans' arrival. The German ration consisted of 300 grams of bread, 250 grams of potatoes, some dehydrated vegetables, and a little margarine. After the first week, sugar was not to be had and soon the margarine supply was exhausted. After three weeks, and in answer to an urgent request, 4,000 Red Cross parcels arrived from Dulag Luft, Wexlar. The Swiss had made arrangements for sending parcels in American convoy and soon parcels began to arrive in GI (Red Cross) trucks.

Throughout this period, large numbers of American POWs were pouring into camp – 1,700 from Stalag Luft 4, 150 a day from Dulag Luft, and finally some men from Oflag 64.

Sanitation was lamentable. The camp was infested with lice, fleas and bedbugs. 3,000 men, each with only 2 filthy German blankets, slept on the bare floors. (Author's Note: this account was not entirely accurate. Many had no blankets and others shared with them. There were some bunks. See following excerpts from "Bulletproof"). Toilet facilities during the day were satisfactory, but the only night latrine was a can in each sleeping barracks. Since many men were still afflicted with diarrhea, the can had an insufficient capacity and the men perforce soiled the floor. Showers were available once every two weeks or not at all. Barracks were not heated and only 200 kilograms of coal were provided for cooking. Morale dropped to its lowest ebb, but Col. Darr Alkire succeeded in maintaining discipline."

Bob Barney, a B-17 pilot whom I met and befriended in Stalag 3, had an infected foot and couldn't make the long march with the rest of us. Instead, he made the entire journey from Sagan to Nuremberg by boxcar, suffering the same horrors as we, but for four days rather than two. In an excellent book titled "Bulletproof," Barney describes his arrival and the conditions at Stalag 13D. The following is an excerpt from Barney's book:

"I was assigned to a barracks at Nuremberg that was next door to an outdoor latrine and washroom. I removed my stinking clothing and washed them in cold water, while shivering against the chill that knifed through me. I hung my clothes to dry on wires strung across the facility and wondered if that were possible in the freezing weather.

I found a few of my friends, including Bob Haverkos and Bob Murphy. Norman Achen, a-P-51 Mustang pilot whom I had known from Stalag Luft III, took me under his wing and helped me get through the clothes-drying period. I gathered the frozen clothes and took them inside, holding them by the stove until they were warm and dry. I dressed and felt almost as good as new. The bandage on my toe was filthy but, upon removal, I noticed that the inside of the bandage remained remarkably clean. The toe, minus a nail, appeared to be mostly healed.

My reunited friends and I compared notes and shared some of our horrifying experiences. My copilot, Lt. O.T. Jones, who I found in another barracks, provided many details. Several Kriegies had collapsed, and were left to perish in the snow. In the weeks ahead, I happily discovered that none of my friends had been among the unfortunate lot who died so miserably. Jones told me that he had come within a whisker of simply giving up. He had discarded his pilot's wings to reduce the weight that he had to carry. I also found that Bill McCarthy, my navigator, had been on the threshold of giving up and nestling down to die in the snow. The terrible lurid details described by those who were on the march were endless and repulsive.

The overall conditions in our Stalag were detailed in a document of protest written by Col. Alkire to the Kommandant. His report, published in a manual titled, West Compound, cited many of the incidents of human abuse in the Nuremberg holding area."

About sleeping conditions, he wrote:

"Many men do not have blankets. Many have no beds of any kind and must sleep on the cold damp floors. At present, there are 1,246 men sleeping on the floors in camps 5, 6, and 7. Stuffing and pallets are vermin-ridden with no replacements and no opportunity to clean those

in use. It is felt that no depot troops of the detaining power are subject to this treatment.

In the new Stalag, it was not uncommon for three men to be assigned to two bunks, resulting in a unique kind of discomfort. A case in point involved Norman Achen, Gene Smith and I sharing two bunks. The uneven mathematics of the accommodations was further complicated by the fact that I had two blankets, and they each had one. Therefore, we pinned them together and remained flat on our backs throughout the night. We cut cards to see who slept in the middle and I turned out to be the unlucky one. We managed to get two upper bunks, side by side, but could not turn over for lack of space.

Despite the sleeping conditions, we considered ourselves fortunate. Many around us slept on the cold floor without blankets. Soon, the entire barracks and our precious blankets were infested with fleas. Eventually, I grew used to them and could lie flat on my back motionless while they crawled over me. For whatever reason, I did not incur many bites. I believe that they utilized me as a bridge en route to Norm and Smitty, because every morning the two of them compared numerous bites, and I remained unbitten. It's a wonder that we coped, but with no other options, we made it work."

At this period in our POW life, food became the most important survival concern. Many who had been prisoners over a few months had lost as much as 20% of body weight, and a number of the less healthy even 25 to 30%. The barracks were especially quiet. Plans for eating, when released, were discussed quietly.

An experience I will never forget would occur when once in a while the goons would provide us with some black bread - a loaf, maybe, for the 13 men in my area. Somehow I had been made unofficial ration officer, thus, I had to cut this loaf into 13 pieces – 13 equal pieces. Then, in agreed order, each person would select their piece – I would get the last piece, which if the largest piece had been selected 12 times before, the 13th piece would be the smallest. The whole process could take a couple of hours. There was no doubt in my mind that my piece was the largest one left and possibly even the largest one when the selection started. There was not a largest piece, but every one wanted to be sure that they didn't get cheated.

That level of hunger is torture and man changes.

XIII

NUREMBERG STALAG LUFT 13D
AND ESCAPE PLAN

By mid-March of 1945, malnutrition and disease, mainly dysentery, had taken a terrible toll on the ever-growing population of POWs now being crammed into the prison at Nuremberg. Energy levels were so low that most of the men, when not standing in line to use the outside latrine by day, or the portable barrel at night, just lay in their bunks. A ghostly silence had descended on the barracks and indeed over the entire Stalag Luft. Fortunately, in spite of the awful food, my digestive system stayed fairly stable but I suffered severely from gingivitis and thought that my teeth might fall out any day.

Deplorable as our situation was, that of the Russian POWs in the adjacent compound was even worse. Through the wire fences they looked like walking skeletons, and daily we could hear their screams and often see them being beaten. We took no comfort in the fact that we weren't being mistreated as badly as the Russians. We only hoped that things didn't get worse for the rest of us.

Although we no longer had access to the BBC broadcasts, word of Allied victories got through to us, mainly from the new POWs being shipped in daily. Our hopes were buoyed by the knowledge that the Allies had penetrated the German homeland and were advancing on all fronts. But the Allied successes also presented a grave danger to us. It was rumored that we were going to be moved again. Word was that we were to be marched south to the Bavarian Alps and hidden in tunnels. There we would be held as hostages while Hitler negotiated with the Allies. The ramifications of both another long march and being held hostage in caves were unthinkable.

Almost every day we could see our giant bombers with their fighter escort passing overhead on their way to pound and destroy the remnants of the Thousand-Year Reich. Often it took over an hour for the armada to pass by and all of us who were able would turn out to watch until the last plane disappeared over the horizon. I suspect that, like me, all were lost in their own dreams of being up there with them. In the few moments of silence that always followed, I know that many prayers were said. Mine was always simple: "Go with God."

Sometimes the bombers targeted the marshalling yards adjacent to Stalag 13D. Although we had great faith in the accuracy of our bombardiers, we worried about strays. So, just to be on the safe side, some of the more nervous POWs dug trenches to jump into when the bombs began to fall. Many of us scoffed at these timid souls until one day a bomb made its way into the compound close to one of the barracks. The size and the population of the trenches quickly doubled. The trenches also filled up when the British bombers hit the marshalling yards. Because they lacked adequate fighter support, the Brits regularly bombed at night with the two-thousand pound bombs known as "blockbusters." In order to avoid bombing the POW camp, a lead aircraft would drop flares on the corners of the marshalling yard to mark the target. It was always an anxious time because the wind often caused the flares to drift, sometimes right over the camp. But thanks to God, and the accuracy of the Brits, none of their bombs came into the compound.

One day, as I was watching the B-24s pass over, a Major whom I knew by sight but had never met or spoken to before, approached and began a conversation. After we chatted for a few minutes, he stepped closer and asked quietly, "Have you thought about escaping?"

Taken off guard by the question and the seriousness of his tone, I laughed nervously and replied, "Haven't we all?"

He smiled at this and I said, "Why do you ask?"

He said, "What do you think the chances are that one could make it?"

I thought about his question. We had been taught that if taken prisoner, our first duty was self-preservation. Another duty was, if at all possible, to attempt to escape. From the day I had been captured, I had considered the possibility as well as the plausibility of escaping. But I always knew that conditions had to be right for any chance of success, and that failure was not a viable option. This had been proven when Hitler ordered the execution of the 50 brave men involved in the "Great Escape."

In my mind there were three conditions, or requirements, for a successful escape: First, you must be physically able, and this requirement alone eliminated a large number of the starved and weakened prisoners; second, you had to have a plan to get outside the prison and out of control of the guards; and finally, you had to have a plan, and the means, to get into friendly hands.

I discussed these thoughts with the Major. I didn't know how long he had been a POW, or how much he knew about the Stalag 3 attempt, so I told him of the chilling effect that the retribution had on all of us. I also pointed out that the conditions since that time had changed.

He stopped me at that point and said that he would like to seriously discuss the possibility of the two of us escaping together. Again, I was taken by surprise. I didn't know why he had chosen me, but the idea was not unappealing. He was a large man who looked to be in reasonably good physical shape. His senior rank indicated maturity and probably a general knowledge and experience beyond mine. If I were to make the attempt, I wanted someone to go with me and this big man looked right. I made a snap decision.

I nodded assent and stuck out my hand, "My name is Norm."

He took my hand and replied, "Call me Moose." He went on, "Norm, this must be just you and me. Don't discuss me, or our conversation, or intentions with anyone."

I said, "Agreed. Let's discuss."

He said, "You alluded to different conditions. We're still in a prison camp. We can't speak German, unless you can. What has changed?"

I pointed out that at Stalag 3, the plan was to get some two hundred men out. This was not a simple plan to cut a hole in the fence and run for it. Rather, it was a very complex plan in which everything had to go right. When two things went wrong, the unanticipated air raid, and the tunnel being twenty feet short and not reaching the trees, the plan began to unravel and things only got worse after that. The Allies had not yet landed on the continent, so even if the attempt had not been detected early, the escapees had to negotiate hundreds of miles through enemy territory to reach the nearest haven in Sweden, Spain, or Switzerland. Thus, those who did make it out of the wire were quickly rounded up, many by German civilians, and the grim retribution began.

The main thing that was different now was the proximity of friendly Allied lines. We still had to be physically able, which I believed both of us were, and we had to find a way to get through the wire and away from the prison camp. But, once away, we wouldn't have to cross the Alps or swim the English Channel to get into friendly hands. The Allied armies were here, in Germany, and from what we had been hearing, maybe within a hundred miles of us.

In this initial discussion we both agreed that present conditions provided us with the possibility of escape. But before we made a final and, very possibly, a fatal decision, there were many things to consider. The rumor that we were going to be moved again persisted and, in fact, gained credibility as the Allies closed in. We decided to think about all the factors involved, whether we stayed put or were moved, and meet again the next day.

We talked several times over the next two weeks, usually while walking back and forth in the exercise area. We discussed the advantages and disadvantages based on the two scenarios. If we were not moved, the probability was that friendly forces would, in the not too distant future, liberate us. There was also the possibility that as the end became inevitable the guards would cut and run, allowing the POWs to leave or stay as we chose. On the other hand, if we were not moved, the odds of a successful escape from the compound were slim at best, and with the deteriorating conditions, if the liberators did not soon arrive, we might all be starved to death.

If we were moved as rumored, there was the prospect of the long march into the Alps. The march from Sagan to Spremburg had been horrible, but this would be worse. The distance was much greater, and the general physical condition of the prisoners had declined. The prospect of being held hostage was even more alarming. The Allies had long proclaimed that their goal was total defeat of the Axis forces - unconditional surrender. After millions had died on both sides pursuing this goal, none of us believed that the Allies would negotiate with Hitler over the fate of the POWs. And all of us believed that Hitler would not hesitate to begin executing prisoners to make his point.

After considering all of these factors, we decided that if we were not moved, we would not attempt to escape. But if we were marched south, as we believed we would be, we would begin the march, wait for the most favorable conditions, and give it our best shot. We would then try to find a place to hide out and wait for our armies to get close before we attempted to make contact.

Stalag 13D, Nuremberg, April 3, 1945, 5 p.m.

Word came down from the German chain of command through the POW chain of command that we were to be prepared to move out at 9 o'clock the next morning; destination: unknown. Each prisoner would be given a Red Cross parcel as we exited the camp. Again we would have no time to integrate the food into our makeshift packs.

Shortly after the order came down, Moose and I met in the exercise area where we could talk privately and re-evaluate our decision to escape.

The first thing Moose said when we met was, "Norm, the time for talk is over. Do you really want to do this?"

I answered quickly, "I do. You?"

Moose nodded, "Most certainly."

We were in concrete. We had discussed this day many times, so we only talked briefly. Since we would probably be in different marching units, I would stay with my group and Moose would find me. We would stay together, watch for an opportunity, and make a dash for it. Once away there was not much we could plan for in advance. We would move north and west where we believed the friendly lines were closest, and react to each situation as it arose. There were so many unknowns, we both felt that this was the only way we could play it.

As I lay in my bunk that night, I was so wound up I barely slept. I felt that Moose and I both knew that we would be safer in the long run if we stayed with the group. But something else was driving us and, lying there in the dark, I concluded that it was a shared competitiveness, a desire to beat these bastards who had starved and mistreated us for so long.

I thought about many things that night. I thought about my wife and mother. I was glad that they didn't know what I was going to do. They would be horrified. I thought about the brave souls who had attempted to escape from Stalag 3 and wondered if we would fare any better. I thought about my comrades who would be making this dreadful march and wondered how many would survive. I thought about God and the part He had played in keeping me alive until now. And would He stay with me? I didn't know how much more I could ask of Him, but I certainly needed Him now and I told Him. Finally, I slept.

At 9 o'clock the next morning, April 4th, we were assembled and ready to march. The prisoners stood in silence, no chatter and very little movement, just weary, near-starved men wondering what was in store for them. Our prisoner chain of command told us that they had been informed that we were headed for Moosburg. But no one had any confidence that the Germans were telling us the truth. We had all heard the stories of how they told the Jews that they were taking them to shower and then they gassed them and buried the bodies in mass graves. And how they had marched the Polish officers into the forest and slaughtered them. The evening before, I'd heard many of my fellow POWs speculating that this might be our fate. This kind of talk only strengthened my resolve to get away as soon as possible. I felt sure that whatever was going to happen, whether it was being gunned down along the way or marched three-hundred kilometers to become hostages, the outcome would not be good. In any case, I didn't plan to stick around to find out.

I wondered how soon Moose and I would find our opportunity to take off. And if we succeeded in breaking away, would they come after us? Moose and I had discussed this many times and had concluded that the guards were stretched too thin and would not be able to pursue. I hoped that this wasn't just wishful thinking.

The men in my barracks were the next to last to leave the camp. Moose was in the last barracks, so would be behind me. A horse-drawn wagon followed the column. It carried the guards' packs and had space for POWs who might not be able to walk. As we went out the gate we were handed a parcel from the back of a Red Cross truck. I was told the drivers were Swiss. As I was handed my parcel, an accented voice said quietly, "Go with God." I was surprised and moved by this gesture of encouragement, particularly since we were under the scrutiny of the guards. I looked up at the man who had handed me the package and, in an equally quiet voice said, "Thank you." He looked steadily ahead and said nothing.

As we marched out the gate I said, "Go with God," to a number of my friends, wondering if I would ever see any of them again in this life. They all said, "Thank you, and you, too." One close friend responded, "I don't know how my connections are with God, but if you hear from him, please put in a good word for me." I don't think that many atheists marched out the gate that day.

About an hour into the march, I realized that I hadn't seen any guard dogs. This was important. If there were no dogs, the probability of pursuit was diminished. I needed to know. I made my way slowly up the column to where our POW group leader was marching. I approached him and asked casually if he knew why there were no dogs. He told me

106

that most of them were lost on the winter march from Sagan because of frozen feet and malnourishment. Many died along the way and many more had to put down at the end of the march.

At about 4 p.m., Moose suddenly appeared beside me, limping and stumbling badly. He said loud enough for those around us to hear, "I can't walk much farther. Would you help me back to the wagon?" I knew that the moment had come. My pulse must have gone to two hundred, and my heart seemed to have moved up into my throat and sounded like a bass drum. I took a couple of deep breaths and stepped out of the column. Moose put his arm around my shoulder and sagged against me for support. I could feel his heart pounding, too. I felt confident at the moment that between us we probably had enough adrenaline pumping to run several miles.

The wagon was about a hundred yards to the rear of the column with one guard aboard holding the reins. The column guard, who was about thirty yards ahead of us, gestured with his weapon and screamed at us to get back in the column. I yelled, "Wagon! Wagon!" Moose pointed at his leg. The guard raised his weapon towards us and I thought that our escape may be over before it began. But the guard must have seen the wagon approaching and believed us, because he abruptly turned and continued marching. The evening was chilly but Moose and I were both dripping sweat.

As the wagon drew alongside, we could see that the driver's head was drooped and his eyes were closed. He was asleep! Everything was right. When the wagon cleared, Moose said, "Now!" and we both took off.

The area bounding the road was thickly wooded and within seconds we were weaving our way through a dense stand of pines and sticky bushes, much underbrush - a thicket. After a few minutes, Moose held his hand up and we stopped to listen. All I could hear was the pounding within. No shots. No shouting. No one in pursuit. We were free, at least for now.

XIV

THE ESCAPE

HEAVY ARTILLERY IN RETREAT
PATTON'S BATTALION OF TANKS

We had probably run four or five hundred yards, but with weaving through the pine thickets and in and out of the brushy areas, we couldn't be at all certain how far we were from our point of departure. We could have easily been moving in a circle back towards the road. In spite of being winded by the sprint, we were both pumped with adrenaline and our instinct was to keep moving as far from the column and our captors as we could. But after a whispered conversation we agreed that it would be best just to hunker down for an hour or so and see what developed. If by then we hadn't detected any pursuit we would plan our next move. We took up a position on the edge of a small clearing where we could see about a hundred yards in the direction that we reckoned pursuit would be most likely. We both sat with our backs against one of the larger pine trees, watching and listening.

The next hour went by ever so slowly. Several times we could hear something moving in the brush which caused us some anxious moments. But nothing sounded big enough to be a human, so we figured it was small animals, probably squirrels hunting for pine nuts. At one point I caught a movement out of the corner of my eye and turned my head just in time to see what must have been a large hare or perhaps a small fox disappear into the thicket some way down the clearing. I sat there for some time picturing a rabbit on a spit over hot coals. It was a vision that would recur many times over the next several days.

After we estimated that about an hour had passed (neither of us had a watch so we could only guess), we decided that we were not being pursued. The guards hadn't detected our departure, or they didn't care enough to do anything about it. Whatever the case, it appeared that the first stage of our escape had been successful and we could begin planning what to do next. Our goal was to find and link up with friendly forces, hopefully the Americans or the British. We knew that the Allied troops had crossed the Rhine, but had no idea where they were now. We had been shocked and somewhat disheartened when we had received news of the near disaster of the Ardennes offensive in December and now prayed that the Germans hadn't mounted another counter-offensive and driven the Allies back out of the Fatherland. We could still hear the big guns far off to the north and west, but didn't know if it was the Red Army or the Americans. We could only hope.

Our immediate concern was what to do next. We debated whether it would be best to keep on the move and try to find our forces, or hold up and wait for them to get closer to us before we tried to make contact. Given that we didn't know where we were, or where we were going, we knew that it would be futile to make any long-range plan. We would just have to see what each day brought and go from there. We concluded that we should try to find a secure hiding place from which we could spend a day or two reconnoitering the area before we settled on our next course of action.

After discussing and agreeing on our "non-plan," we hid our packs in a dense thicket and began a systematic reconnaissance of our immediate area to find out what we were into and how to get out of it. The sky was overcast, but we could see a dim glow of the sun from which we got a western bearing and calculated that we had about two hours of daylight left. We knew that we'd come from the east so we went west for about a hundred yards then, starting north, made a quarter-circle back to our packs.

Having found nothing but more thicket, we went back to the west and made a quarter-circle south and back to our base point. Same result - no trails, roads or any other sign of human penetration. We repeated the maneuver but this time went out about two hundred yards. Still nothing.

We discussed splitting up and exploring separately so as to cover more ground before dark, but decided it was a bad idea. Truth was, we were both scared and the thought of getting separated was even more frightening. We stayed together.

We figured we had time for one more search. This time we planned to go south for about five hundred yards, then circle back to the north for about half a mile, and then back south until we found our base. About a quarter of a mile out on the southern leg, we came upon a dirt road running east and west. We assumed that it joined the road from which we had escaped our captors. We paralleled the road west for two or three hundred yards until it curved slightly and in the distance we could see a bridge spanning a stream that ran generally north to south. There was a shack that appeared to be a guardhouse on the near side. We couldn't tell if it was manned or not, so we cautiously turned back north and, staying well in the woods, followed the stream until it turned in an easterly direction. At that point we headed back to the southeast until we found the small clearing and the thicket where we'd stashed our packs.

All things considered, we felt good about our immediate situation. Our hiding place seemed to be secure and, from our reconnaissance, we knew that there was water nearby and a road leading in the direction which we wanted to go, if and when we decided to move. Moose had squirreled away a few sheets of paper and the nub of a pencil so we were able to draw up a rough map of our area with the routes we'd taken and what we'd found.

By the time we had finished the map it was getting dark, so we raked up a mattress of pine needles and, since we each had a blanket, laid one down on the pine needles and put one over us. The April night was chilly but not terribly cold so we were reasonably comfortable.

Before we bedded down, we developed a nighttime warning system. If one of us heard something or sensed danger of any sort, we were to place a hand and press lightly on the shoulder or upper torso of the other. This meant "Lie still and listen." That first night I lay awake for a long time and must have heard a hundred noises that raised the hackles on my neck and tempted me to use our alert system. But after a while I came to the conclusion that the noises were just the birds and squirrels moving about and eventually I dozed off. Sometime later I felt a hand on my shoulder and immediately became simultaneously alert and frightened. I lay dead still, not even breathing, and shortly heard "hooo, hooo" from somewhere nearby. A moment later there was a "hooo, hooo" from another direction. It sounded like someone signaling - two people letting each other know where they were. I thought, "My God. It's a search party. They've discovered us missing and are looking for us." We lay frozen, waiting for our captors to break into our thicket and pounce on us. But after some thirty minutes, when no one appeared and we heard no more hooting, we concluded that our "search party" was a couple of owls in the first stages of courtship. I eventually got my breathing and heart rate under control, but to this day I get a chill when I hear an owl hoot.

At first light, we made our way back towards the dirt road we'd discovered the previous evening. We felt a little more secure about our bearings now so we felt that, as long as we stayed in known territory, we could split up for short periods. When we reached the road, Moose turned east to see if the dirt road did indeed go back and intersect the road we'd escaped from, and if so, what kind of traffic was on it: military, civilian, farmers, refugees, or what. From the volume and type of traffic we thought we might get a feel for how close our Allied armies were. In reality, we were hoping that we would find a column of G.I.s in hot pursuit of the fleeing Germans and our fellow POWs. Meanwhile, staying in the edge of the woods on the north side of the road, I headed toward the bridge to see if I could determine whether or not it was guarded. We planned to meet back at our parting spot in what we would estimate to be two hours. Since we were pretty certain that there were owls in the area we decided that two short hoots and a long "hoooo" meant that there was danger along the road. If one of us gave the signal, the other was to leave the road and go as quickly as possible back to our thicket.

When I reached the bend in the road from which we'd first seen the bridge, I lay down and watched for a while. The bridge and shack were about a hundred-fifty yards down the road. The shack looked to be about eight by eight with a door facing the road and a small, chest-high window facing east down the road where approaching traffic could be observed. I assumed that there was a similar window on the bridge side. After about thirty minutes, in which I'd seen no movement either along the road or around the shack, I decided to move closer to a better vantage point. I moved carefully through the woods on the north side of the road until I came to a thicket of smaller pines which afforded me good cover. I climbed about fifteen feet up in the branches of a sturdy-looking tree and sat on a limb where I had a clear view of the shack, the bridge and the road. I had just settled in when a man stepped out of the shack and started walking east on the road. He wore an odd-looking uniform, the likes of which I hadn't seen before, and was armed with some kind of an ancient rifle slung over his left shoulder. He walked at a kind of shamble east on the road right past my hiding place in the tree. I could see he was an old man and, from that and his uniform, I guessed that he was one of the "Home Guard." These were Germans who, because they had been wounded in battle or were too old to fight in regular units, were conscripted for local guard duties. Not the SS, but still dangerous to unarmed, escaped prisoners. He continued on down the road and it occurred to me that he was patrolling and would go on to the intersection of the main road where he might stumble upon Moose, who would be watching in the other direction. I tried to let out a hoot to warn Moose but my throat was constricted and all I got was a croak - more like a frog than an owl. I took some deep breaths and was about to try again when the guard reached the curve in the road and stopped. He watched down the road for a few moments and then turned and started back towards the bridge. When he was nearly abreast of my position he turned abruptly into the woods and stopped almost directly below me. I froze and held my breath, hoping he wouldn't look up or that I wouldn't faint from fright or lack of oxygen and fall out of the tree. I mouthed a silent prayer that as I recall went something like, "Oh, dear God, please help me out here. Surely you didn't bring me through all of this just to be shot out of a tree by an old man with a blunderbuss!" The old man leaned his rifle against my tree, lit a cigarette, recovered his rifle, and headed back towards the guardhouse.

When I could breathe again, I climbed carefully down from the tree and made my way back through the woods to our designated rendezvous point. Moose showed up about thirty minutes later and I recounted my reconnaissance, detailing the bridge, the guardhouse, and the guard, but leaving out the parts about how I had tried unsuccessfully to warn him and the minor anxieties I'd suffered.

Moose said that his exploration had confirmed that our dirt road did link up with the main north-south road as we had thought, and that a good number of what appeared to be refugees were moving south. He said that there was no traffic heading north and he had not seen any German soldiers.

When we got back to our thicket, we assessed our situation. The heavy refugee movement south seemed to verify our assumption that an Allied force was bearing down from the north. In all probability, that would be the Russians. The lack of any refugee movement to the west led us to believe, or hope, that perhaps the Americans or the Brits were closing in from that direction. In any case, we decided that our best course was to stay put, keep watching the roads, and see what developed.

We spent the next couple of hours building a low profile lean-to from sticks we gathered and small pine boughs we were able to whittle off with a folding knife that Moose had in his pack. It was about two feet high at the open front, sloping to eighteen inches or so at the rear. We cut three small firs which we placed at the opening. All in all, we thought it was a superior job and that it would provide us good concealment and adequate protection from the elements.

The question was how long could we hold out there? We had water nearby that we could make drinkable with iodine, which we had, so the critical item was food. We did an analysis of our supply and what we needed each day to sustain us. We calculated that we had enough to last for four days on a prudent diet and up to eight days on a near-starvation diet. Our dilemma was that if we took the starvation diet and our troops didn't get near within eight days, we might not have enough strength to move on. We considered alternatives. Our explorations hadn't turned up any potential sources such as farms with crops or barnyards with chickens and we had no means to trap birds or small animals. We thought about the stream and the possibility that it might have fish in it, but couldn't think of any way to catch them. We decided to compromise and ration what we had to last six days. If by then no one had reached us, we would have to cross the canal and move to the west.

That night I lay awake for some time thinking about how we could get any kind of nourishment. As a kid from the country, I'd learned about edible roots and berries and even some types of leaves and grasses. But we were in a pine forest, and pine needles weren't edible. The thickets of brush didn't look promising either. Then I remembered that I'd seen snails alongside the stream. I wondered if we could eat them. I shuddered at the thought, but I didn't dismiss it. I had eaten raw oysters a number of times, but always smothered with catsup and horseradish.

The next morning, I mentioned the snails to Moose. After some thought he said, "What the hell, let's try it." We made our way over to the stream and gathered up about a dozen snails. We rinsed them in iodine water and then tried to figure out the best way to get them out of the shells. After trying several methods we discovered, quite by accident, that if we blew softly into the shell they would poke their head out and we could scoop the meat out with Moose's penknife.

I popped the first one in my mouth and swallowed quickly. I nearly gagged, and it tasted pretty awful, but it went down. Moose tried one with about the same result. Then he came up with the idea of preceding the snail with a small piece of chocolate and that worked pretty well. We had no idea of the nutritional merit of the snails, but we knew that they must have some value as a supplement to our meager food supply and, if nothing else, reduced our hunger for a while.

But even with these added morsels, hunger was our constant companion. I'd been told that over a period of time the body adjusts to a starvation diet and I guess mine had, because I was still functioning. I had also been told that if all of a sudden you eat more than your starved system has adjusted to, you would throw it up and, if you continued to eat, you could possibly kill yourself. Eat yourself to death! It was a thought I pondered quite often and thought that, if I ever reached civilization again, I might test the theory.

It was obvious to both Moose and me that when we escaped, we put ourselves in a much different and more dangerous situation. If SS, or Gestapo or Hitler Youth found us, we would for sure be killed. Probably that could be true with a lot of Luftwaffe and civilians. Our only sure safety would be with our own troops. We were so tense and alert that by day we knew we needed other mental challenges and Moose provided that with a new book he had received from his sister and had carried with him. "The Razor's Edge," by Somerset Maugham, had just been published in the United States. We escaped into this book like hungry wolves and quickly found out we had much to discuss and learn. Larry, the character in the book whom we found deep emotion for, had been a fighter pilot in WWI. Some experience or experiences that he had never identified had directed him toward getting some answers, if answers were available: What is the purpose of life? Is there a God? Did we know that before we needed Him? Both Moose and I said we believed in God, but had trouble describing the way we believed in Him. Every day as we discussed and asked questions in our whispered conversation, we learned a lot about what we didn't know.

One day towards the end of our stay in this thicket, I asked Moose what form we would be in Heaven. He gave that some serious thought and finally said, "As souls."

I thought about this for some time and then asked him again, "Are you going to be happy for eternity to be a soul?"

His immediate response was, "Certainly, as long as there are female souls."

Of course I had to ask, "How are you going to tell a female soul from a male soul?"

"Easy," he said, "she will smell better."

This was the very first time I had laughed all the way down to my toes since I had left England. And today when I write this, 60 years later, I hope Moose was right. She will smell better.

Early in the morning on our fourth day out, we heard a siren coming from some distance to the west, which we assumed to be an air raid warning. Shortly after that we heard people talking nearby. We crawled into our hideout and waited to see if they were coming our way. We stayed hunkered down for fifteen or twenty minutes and we could still hear the voices but they didn't seem to be getting any closer, so we crept out of our lair just in time to see a massive flight of B-24s and B-17s moving towards the heart of Germany in a formation that must have been ten miles long. Crisscrossing above and below, like shepherds watching over their flocks, were our beloved Mustangs. I wanted to jump up and down and shout, but knew that would not be prudent under present conditions. I just stood there looking skyward and murmuring, "Go with God. Go with God..." When the last bomber had disappeared, I looked over at Moose. That big, strong man was standing, still looking skyward, with tears streaming down his face. I was not ashamed that my face was also wet.

Some two hours later, the armada was again overhead, this time heading for England. Shortly after the last planes disappeared to the west we heard the all-clear signal and became aware that we could no longer hear the people talking. We waited for about thirty minutes and then carefully moved in the direction from which we'd heard the voices. In a small clearing about two hundred yards east of our hideout we found fresh tracks and cigarette butts. It looked as if someone was using the woods as an air raid shelter. This was puzzling. We didn't think it was Germans because we had been told that most of the rural people had cellars that they used for shelters. Then, who?

Two days later the sirens sounded and again we heard the voices. We decided to investigate. We moved cautiously through the woods to where we could see the clearing. On the far side of the little clearing were six men sitting under the pines smoking and talking. They were all dressed in tattered clothes and looked to be not quite emaciated, but very thin. I immediately thought of the Russian prisoners across the fences at Nuremberg. I was sure they had to be slave laborers and, after listening for a few minutes, decided that they were probably Russians, but had no idea where they'd come from. I tapped Moose on the shoulder and we retreated to where we could whisper without being heard. Moose had also concluded that they were Russians. We didn't know if we could trust them, but our scant supply of food was almost gone and neither of us felt like we could face another snail, so we decided to gamble.

We entered the clearing with our arms out to our sides in a non-menacing manner and said, "Americans. Americans."

They all looked startled and for a few anxious moments there was dead silence. Then one of them, the closest to us, said, "Americans." He turned to the others and repeated "Americans." He then turned back to us and gesturing toward himself and his comrades said, "Russians."

Not knowing what to do next, I stepped forward and stuck out my hand. Their spokesman took it and pumped it vigorously. Then they all came forward and shook our hands and patted us on the back, all of them smiling broadly and repeating, "Americans. Americans."

For the next half-hour or so, until the all-clear sounded, we communicated as best we could in sign language and drawings on the ground. We got across that we were escaped prisoners and they let us know that they were prisoners also, working at forced labor in a factory about two kilometers to the north. They indicated that when there was an air raid, the Germans went to bunkers, leaving the laborers to shift for themselves, so they ran into the woods and gathered at this clearing until the all-clear was sounded. We told them that we had been hiding in these woods for several days and badly needed food. We were purposely vague about our hiding place.

They moved a short distance away and talked together for a few minutes and I could see that there was some disagreement. Two of them were shaking their heads and I could hear them saying, "Nyet" - one of the few words I understood. But in the end we must have passed muster, because the spokesman came to us and indicated they would help us out. He pointed at us, and then himself, and then brought his hands together and pointed at the ground we were standing on. I mimicked his gestures, nodded and said, "Da" to indicate I understood we were to meet here. He then pointed at the sun, moved his hand slowly down to the horizon and drew a "plus one" on the ground. I was puzzled for a moment, but this time Moose nodded and said, Da" and to me, "They'll meet us here one hour after sundown." We all shook hands again and parted.

We felt pretty confident our new-found friends would not betray us, but to be on the safe side we were hidden where we could watch the clearing a good half-hour before the designated meeting time. We had been there about twenty minutes when we heard someone whistle and a lone figure stepped into the clearing. In the gathering darkness we couldn't tell whether or not it was one of the Russians we'd met earlier that day. It crossed my mind that we could be stepping into a trap. But we had come this far, we were hungry to the point of desperation and we had no choice. I motioned to Moose to stay put and went forward into the clearing. I had to get close before I recognized the man as one of our Russian friends. It was not the spokesman - in fact, I thought it was one of the men who had seemed to argue against helping us. This made me a little nervous. But he handed me a small cloth bundle and put his hand on my shoulder and squeezed gently. I returned the gesture. He then indicated that one of them would meet us at the same time and place the next day. I was trying to thank him when, without another word, he touched my shoulder again, turned and disappeared into the woods.

Moose had moved quietly up beside me and we both stood for a few moments watching the woods into which our benefactor had disappeared. We opened the bundle and inside were two boiled potatoes and two slices of black bread. On the way back to our shelter I thought about what had just taken place. This food had to have been taken from these Russian prisoners' own barely life-sustaining rations. I was quite sure that anyone caught sneaking the food out would pay a heavy penalty - probably in front of a firing squad. They had given up their precious food and the man who delivered it had certainly risked his life for us - two American strangers. I put him in the same category as the Fraulein and the German mother who had saved my life on the day I "landed" on German soil. I truly believed that God stepped in again, through these miserable Russian slaves, to save my life and, either coincidentally or by design, that of my companion, Moose. I believe that to this day.

Sometime in the wee hours of our thirteenth night of "freedom," Moose awakened me with our squeeze of the shoulder warning signal. I was instantly alert. Moose whispered, "Do you hear that?" I listened for a few moments and far off to the south and west I could hear heavy equipment moving. We lay silent, listening for ten or fifteen minutes. As the sound of movement grew louder, we could tell that vehicles, a lot of vehicles, were moving east along the dirt road to our south. About that time we heard the rumble of heavy equipment crossing the bridge – first the thump, thump of trucks, and then the distinct clanking and grinding of tracked vehicles, probably tanks. It didn't take long to figure out that this was a military convoy of some kind.

The movement went on for several hours. The head of the convoy had reached the main road to the east of us and we assumed had turned south.

Just before dawn, the vehicle movement stopped and now we could hear a lot of yelling – we assumed orders being shouted – and not in English. We decided to investigate.

We cautiously made our way to a point where we could see the road, and as it began to get light, we were astounded to see German self-propelled artillery interspersed with trucks all up and down the road and into the wood line to the south of the road. The vehicles in the woods had their guns – which appeared to be 90-mm cannons – deployed in a firing mode, pointed to the north and west. We counted twenty-five gun-mounted vehicles just in the area that we could observe. Many of the soldiers had gotten out of their vehicles and were milling around, so we scurried back to our thicket.

We were exhilarated. We were certain that this was the German army, the Thousand-Year Reich, in retreat. And that meant that the Allies must be closing in. We were somewhat anxious about having German soldiers so close by, but figured and hoped that they wouldn't stray this far into the woods.

The Germans stayed in place all that day. The big guns fired sporadically to the north and west, the direction from which we assumed our forces were advancing. Every thirty minutes or so one of the big rounds would go directly over our position. The whoosh-whoosh-whoosh sounded like a freight train going by and kept us alert and tense.

About mid-afternoon the firing stopped, and we could hear the troops shouting and laughing all up and down the road. It sounded like they were partying. We hadn't heard anyone moving around in our vicinity, so we crawled out of our lean-to and sat listening to the apparent festivities going on down at the road. This was a careless and near-fatal mistake on our part.

We were so absorbed in what was going on at the road that we were taken totally off guard when a German soldier stumbled out of the woods directly in front of us, not ten yards away. Stunned, we both froze momentarily. The soldier stood swaying, looking right at us. I could see that he was having trouble focusing. He was drunk! He was also unarmed. I rose to a crouch, prepared to spring at him if he moved toward us or let out a cry. But he turned abruptly and went back in the direction he'd come from. Moose and I retreated quickly into our shelter and pulled fresh pine branches, which we'd cut that morning, over the opening. We knew that he had seen us but there was nothing we could do. With German soldiers all around it would be suicide to try to move. All we could do was wait and hope that the soldier was drunk enough that it hadn't registered what he'd seen. I also petitioned the Lord again, and I think I detected Moose doing the same.

Fifteen or twenty anxious minutes went by. Then we heard someone approaching. Peering out through the pine boughs I could see that our drunken soldier had returned, and this time he was armed and had another soldier with him. They approached and stood not 30 feet from the entrance to our hideout, talking loudly. I didn't dare move, even my head, so I could only see their legs. The drunken soldier was stumbling around, swaying badly, and I was terrified that he was going to fall on top of us. They stayed there apparently arguing for two or three minutes and then moved on. When we could breathe again we talked about the incident and guessed that the sober soldier figured that his drunken friend was hallucinating. Someone was taking care of us!

Late that afternoon, we heard a lot of shouting and, shortly after that, engines cranked up and vehicles began moving. We assumed the German retreat was continuing. The movement went on for an hour or so until all of the convoy had apparently reached the main north-south road and headed south. We waited until just before dark and then ventured out and moved cautiously to where we could see the dirt road and the bridge. As we had suspected, the road was deserted and the guards were gone from the bridge.

A hasty check of the area turned up a lot of trash including some discarded black bread, which we gathered up and put in a small cloth sack we'd found. We were hoping that some careless soldier had left his weapon, or perhaps a grenade lying around, but we didn't find anything of that sort.

We returned to the thicket and assessed our situation. We assumed that with the German artillery in retreat, the armor and infantry would not be far behind. We discussed our options. At first we thought that it might be safer to stay put and wait for the German front line units to pass by. But then it occurred to us that the artillery may have redeployed a couple of miles down the road, well within range of the river and beyond, and we knew enough about ground war tactics to figure out that if the Germans were fighting a delaying action, the river would make a good defensive position. This raised the possibility of German soldiers deployed along our side of the river and spread out through the woods around us. That in itself was alarming, but even scarier was the thought of Allied artillery and close support aircraft pounding the riverbank and the surrounding woods. Our lean-to provided good concealment but would not protect us from bombs and artillery rounds. And another, perhaps even more significant factor dominated our thinking - we were tired of waiting. We decided it was time to move.

We bundled up our blankets and what food we had and, wearing all of our clothes, began what we hoped would be the last leg of our odyssey. We made our way to the dirt road and, in the faint light of a half-moon, partially obscured by a thin layer of clouds, crossed the bridge and headed west.

We stayed on the road, prepared to duck into the woods alongside at the first sign of trouble. A mile or so after we crossed the bridge, the road turned to the north and by then the clouds had dissipated and visibility was good. About three hours out we saw in the distance what seemed to be a small village. We stopped to assess the situation. We could see only a couple of lights on and figured that at this time of night, ten o'clock or thereabout, there wouldn't be anybody out moving around. We thought about skirting the village, but the area was heavily forested and if we struck out through the woods, at best we would lose a lot of valuable night traveling time, and at worst might get lost – end up God knows where. We decided to stay on the road and take our chances.

We made it through the village all right, but on the far side, we came around a turn in the road and saw several people walking towards us. We ducked into the woods, not knowing whether we'd been seen or not. About a hundred yards off the road we climbed a small hill with enough opening that we could see the road and part of the village. We decided to watch for a while and see if anybody came after us.

Shortly after we watched the walkers disappear into the village, we heard an engine start up and a motorcycle came tearing out of the village past the point where we had just left the road. We couldn't tell for sure, but it looked like the motorcycle had a sidecar with a passenger in it. After the motorcycle passed, we moved further from the road and came across a well-used dirt road running generally east to west. We could hear the motorcycle now going back and forth on the road and figured that they must be looking for us. Assuming that at first light a search party might start scouring the woods in the area, we decided we had better move on. We got on the dirt road and headed west.

We stayed on the road, which climbed steadily for the next several miles. We could see cut trees along both sides and concluded that we were on a logging road... probably originating in the village we'd passed through. About midnight, the road leveled out and turned to the north. We came around a corner into a clearing that in the moonlight looked to be several hundred yards across. We had just taken a few steps into the clearing when we saw a blinking signal light in the far wood-line. We moved rapidly back into the woods. About that time a hound started baying and we could hear raised voices. We had no idea what we had run in to, but it didn't sound good. We quickly discussed the situation and concluded that it must be a German military unit, probably light artillery, that they had a bloodhound, that the hound had probably picked up our scent, and that we had better get the hell out of there – now!

We moved as quickly and quietly as we could back down the road to a bridge we'd crossed spanning a small mountain stream. In the middle of the bridge we jumped over the side into the water and took off downstream. We figured that, if they came after us, the hound would follow our scent back over the bridge and on down the road from which we'd come – at least we hoped that's what would happen.

The water was little more than ankle-deep but ice-cold and the rocky streambed made the going rough. We stayed in the stream for several hundred yards before we emerged on the far side and stopped to listen. We could hear the hound barking, but the yelps seemed to be getting farther away so we guessed that our ruse had worked and that the Huns and the hound had gone on down the road.

Our feet were numb from the icy water. I wanted to sit down and take my boots off and rub my feet to see if I could get some circulation going but Moose said we ought to keep moving for a while and I knew he was right. We followed the stream down for about an hour until we came to a huge boulder with an overhang that created a sort of small cave. After cautiously checking to make sure it wasn't occupied by local denizens, we crawled in and, with wet boots still on in case we had to make a run for it, wrapped ourselves in our blankets like two peas in a pod and tried to sleep. But, exhausted as I was, my feet hurt so bad I couldn't sleep. Both feet had been frostbitten on the march from Sagan and, now that the numbness was wearing off, they felt like they were on fire. I laid there in agony and, for the first time since we'd made our escape, I felt that if the Germans found us, I would give up without a fight – I just couldn't run anymore.

But the Germans didn't find us and the morning brought wonderful warming sunshine and renewed spirits. We decided we were reasonably safe in our little haven so, with some difficulty, we took our nearly frozen boots off and let our nearly frozen feet thaw out. With an hour or so of sunshine and a lot of massaging, we were ready to move on.

We followed the stream in a southerly direction for about a mile until we came to a place where we could cross on boulders without getting our feet frozen again. From there we put the sun at our back and, for the next couple of hours, headed west through pine forested rolling hill country. From the position of the sun, I guessed it was about ten o'clock when we topped one of the highest hills in the area. The forest had thinned considerably and we could see a dirt road a few hundred yards down in the valley below that led to a small village at the north end of the valley. The valley appeared to be about a half-mile across and quite open. Plenty of space to run but no place to hide. On the far side of the valley was another series of forested ridgelines similar to the ones which we had just crossed.

We watched the road for fifteen or twenty minutes and didn't see any traffic, so we decided to go on down across the road and, with as much energy as we could muster, make a dash across the open valley and continue on to the west.

We started down the slope but had only made it about fifty yards when a German half-track came roaring up the road heading for the village. There were two men in the vehicle, a driver and a soldier, standing, manning a mounted weapon that we later decided was a 20mm cannon. We were caught in the open so we froze in place, hoping they wouldn't see us. But just as they came about abreast of our position, the gunner pointed towards us. We spun around and scampered back towards the woods. The half-track didn't stop but the gunner got off two shots in our direction. One hit well down the slope behind us and then the gunner over-adjusted and the next one whistled over our heads and exploded in the treetops on the ridge. Neither was close enough to hurt us but the overall effect revived our adrenaline flow and greatly improved our foot-speed.

When we got into the woods we moved about a quarter-mile south to get away from the place where we'd last been seen. As we walked along the ridgeline, the half-track, now loaded with soldiers, came back down the road and sped on south. It looked to us like a hasty evacuation. If so, it was good news.

We found a spot where the sun filtered through the trees and, exhausted from the run and the flow and ebb of adrenaline, took off our still-wet boots and outer layers of clothing, flopped down and promptly fell asleep.

It must have been around noon when Moose roused me. My clothes were pretty well dry and warm when I put them on. I felt refreshed and hopeful – a hundred and eighty degrees from the night before. Moose said he'd had a good sleep, too, and was ready to move on.

In high spirits and with renewed vigor, we hiked on down the slope, crossed the now-deserted road and made our way quickly across the valley and into the wood-line on the other side. We stayed as best we could on a westerly course, zigzagging to avoid heavy pine thickets and brushy barriers. Sometime about mid-afternoon we came out of our woods on what appeared to be a deserted autobahn. We wanted to cross… needed to cross… but it was at least 150 yards to the trees on the opposite side and we were extremely cautious. We had already lucked out more than we wanted to. Before we could make our dash-or-not decision, from our right, maybe two miles or more, came a small airplane flying at about one thousand feet and in a criss-cross pattern that would take him a half-mile in front of us. As he got closer, I recognized that it was an L-5 observation plane used by our ground forces to fly in front to spot problems – at about this same time we heard the low roar of tanks. They were probably a mile or even two behind the L-5, but there were a lot of them. A quick explanation to Moose and we were off running to meet our friends before they could get by us.

At some point before we reached our new target we heard from our right, "Halt. Halt!" in German. This only stimulated both Moose and me to up to highest gear. No shots and I have no reason to say why not.

As we approached the frontage road, the L-5 had already passed us but not the tanks. We slowed down and walked out to the side of the road with our hands up. About four hundred yards to our right, coming toward us, were American Sherman Tanks and, as we watched, the cannon on each tank swung slowly to aim at us. It is a sight that I will never forget but I am thankful I have not dreamed about it for several years.

A jeep pulled out from the formation – besides the driver, there was a Major and a soldier behind a mounted 50-caliber machine gun. We yelled, "Escaped American POWs! We need your help." The Major was continually on his radio. He finally waved to us to put down our hands and the column of tanks started to roll forward. The cannons swung

124

toward the front as they passed and in the cupola the tank Commander saluted us.

The Major in the jeep told us to stay put and a jeep would soon be by to pick us up. As he moved off to rejoin the column he, too, saluted us. As I saluted in return, a new emotion trickled down my face.

XV

PARIS AND THE RITZ

I can barely begin to describe the myriad emotions that engulfed me as we stood there waiting for our jeep and watching the American tanks roll by: utter happiness, relief and, perhaps more than anything, pride. These conquering heroes were saluting us, Moose and me! We were bone-weary, filthy, tattered, and starved, but we were no longer prisoners. We were American soldiers and these magnificent fighting men were honoring us. I stood straight and proud as I returned each salute.

We must have waited thirty or forty minutes before the jeep came by and picked us up. Twice during that time the column came to a halt and the tanks deployed to the sides of the road. The first time the tanks stopped, we could hear machine gun fire off toward the head of the column. The second time, two of the tanks near us fired their machine guns, and then several rounds from their main guns, to the east in the direction from which we'd just come. We couldn't see what they were firing at, but were later told they had been fired on and had returned fire. It was probably the Germans who had yelled at us as we sprinted for the autobahn.

After the last of the tanks passed by, a jeep pulled over and picked us up. The driver was a corporal and the passenger a staff sergeant. Neither of them looked like they were more than nineteen or twenty. At twenty-three I felt, and must have looked to them, like an old man. The sergeant asked us if we needed water and offered his canteen. We both drank. He then produced a K-ration pack, which we greedily tore apart and then began opening the tins with the little can opener that comes with the packets. In my haste, I cut my finger on one of the tins and Moose said that maybe I'd get a purple heart out of all of this after all. Moose and I roared at this and our benefactors laughed politely, probably not understanding the irony.

We followed the column for several miles to where the tanks were in the process of coiling into defensive positions in and around a small village. We were taken to what appeared to be the only hotel in town, now occupied by the headquarters of the tank battalion. The commander of the tank battalion, a Lieutenant Colonel, who in turn introduced us to his staff, met us there. They all greeted us warmly and treated us with great respect. After the introductions, the Battalion Commander took us aside and asked us from which direction we'd come and if we'd seen any large German units or anything else that might be of intelligence value. We described our escape route as best we could, told him about the unit with the dog and what we believed to be the mechanized unit retreating south from the village we'd passed by the day before. He thanked us for the information and told us that he was going out to check his units' night positions, and that we were free to get cleaned up and find the kitchen. He called one of his Lieutenants over and told him to see that we were taken care of. We thanked the Commander and he left to make his rounds. The Lieutenant took us in tow and showed us the kitchen and dining area, the two community bathrooms in the hotel and the two rooms that had been designated for us.

The cleaning up process took a good bit of time. There was no hot water and we had several layers of German soil that we'd accumulated along the way. Shaving presented another challenge. Our one razor had given out long ago and the straight razor provided by the hotel wasn't much sharper than Moose's pocketknife. Given that, the cold water, and a sliver of soap that produced very little lather, I considered leaving the beard. But when I looked in the mirror I knew it had to go. Like the filth I'd just washed off and the tattered clothes I still wore, it seemed to me a symbol of our captivity and flight and I wanted to be done with it. Somehow I got it scraped off. When I later remarked to Moose that I wished we could find a barber, he offered to cut my hair with the straight razor. I declined. The haircut would have to wait.

After cleaning up, we made our way to the dining area. A couple who appeared to be in their sixties and whom we later found out were the owners, served us a delicious potato soup and black bread that didn't taste like sawdust. The Battalion officers, who'd apparently already eaten, had discovered the hotel's wine cellar and were in the process of liberating and consuming what they could of the contents. Somehow, someone had

127

also found and "liberated" a covey of French ladies whom I was told had been brought to Germany as slave laborers. Judging by their youth and good looks, I wondered just what sort of slave labor they'd been called upon to perform, but I didn't ask. At any rate, it looked like it was going to be a night of celebration and the "emancipated" French girls seemed to be having as much fun as anybody. Moose and I were invited to join in and I was tempted, but reluctantly declined. I felt that putting alcohol in my system would not be a good idea, and besides, I was dead tired, totally drained physically and mentally. I said goodnight and headed for my room. One of the officers stopped me and told me that he didn't know how, or with whom, I would be traveling for the next few days, but that I needed to protect myself. He gave me a pistol - an Italian Beretta that I still have to this day.

I slept like a stone. When I woke up and looked out the window the next morning, the tanks, which had been parked along a brick wall that enclosed a cemetery nearby, were gone. I checked Moose's room, which was next to mine, and found that he was gone, too. Somewhat alarmed that I'd been forgotten and left behind, I stuck the Beretta in my waistband and ventured down the hallway. The rooms that had been occupied by the battalion officers were deserted. I went down to the kitchen area where I found no one but the old couple who had served us the night before. They were obviously overwhelmed and somewhat frightened by all that had been going on. They offered me breakfast and told me as best they could that the Americans would be back. The smell of coffee and bacon cooking eclipsed my fears of being deserted and I accepted their kind offer.

While I was enjoying my first real breakfast in many months, I heard a vehicle pull up outside. Shortly thereafter, Moose, the Major who had been in the lead jeep the day before and a young lady, whom Moose introduced as "Fifi," came in. Moose came over and clapped me on the back and said he was glad I was back among the living. He and the Major both laughed at this and Moose said, "Are you ready to take on Paris?"

I didn't know if he was serious or kidding, but I said, "Why not?"

The car that had been 'liberated' to take us to Paris was an elegant-looking, older convertible which, the Major told us, had belonged to a very unpopular local Nazi official who had mysteriously disappeared just before the American tanks rolled into town. I don't know what make it was, but it reminded me of the car I'd seen in newsreels back home

128

carrying a confident-looking President waving at cheering crowds lining the sides of the streets. In the back seat there were two cases of K-rations, a case of assorted liquor (which turned out to be Hennessy Five Star and Courvoisier), and two cans of gasoline. Compared to what we'd been used to, it looked like enough supplies to last for a month.

The Major also gave us a map on which he had highlighted what he considered the best and safest route to the Rhine River. From there he told us we would have to get further directions to Nancy, France, and then on to Paris. He cautioned us that although there were Allied support units strung out all along the way to the Rhine, the forward tank units had moved so fast they had bypassed many small pockets of resistance that could be very dangerous to a lone civilian car traveling the roads. We thanked the Major and assured him that we would be careful, as we had no desire to become POWs again.

An hour later we were on the road: Moose, me, and Fifi, whom Moose described as our guide and interpreter. I wasn't sure how Fifi was going to be of much help since she didn't speak any English, wasn't much at reading a map, and had no idea how to get to Paris. But she was a bubbly girl, obviously happy to be on her way home, and her lack of language skills didn't deter her from taking her guide duties seriously with a lot of talking and pointing. So, with Moose driving, me reading the map, and Fifi and I giving directions and watching for the enemy, we were on our way to Paris.

As it turned out the map, the directions, our "guide," and most of the supplies, were superfluous. We had traveled west for just over an hour on nearly deserted roads when we spotted several tanks at a crossroad just ahead. We recognized them as American tanks and breathed a grateful sigh of relief. Moose slowed the vehicle and I stood up and raised my hands in the air as we approached. We sure didn't want to get shot up by our own troops. Two of the soldiers got down from the tanks and, with weapons at the ready, signaled for us to stop. One of the soldiers, a sergeant, approached the car and asked us if we spoke English. I told him that we were escaped POWs, described briefly how we'd gotten there and told him that we were on our way to liberate Paris. He just grinned and said that he was pretty sure that Paris had already been liberated, but that we were welcome to continue on and see for ourselves. He told us that we would soon begin encountering Allied logistical units that were headquartered in a town four or five miles to the west. We thanked him and drove on.

129

Within a few minutes after leaving the crossroad, we started seeing tanks deployed alongside the road and out into the fields and tree lines nearby. By the time we entered the town that the sergeant had mentioned, the military traffic was heavy, mostly with supply trucks and fuel tankers. In the center of town an M.P. stopped us and asked us who the hell we were, and where the hell did we think we were going? I gave him basically the same explanation I'd given before: that we were Air Force Officers, escaped POWs, and that we were headed for Paris. As I was explaining, he was examining the car and its contents, paying particular attention to the two cases of brandy, and the French girl.

When I had finished with my explanation he asked, "And I suppose this young lady is also an escaped POW?"

I had no good answer for this so I looked at Moose, who just shrugged. Apparently, he had no good answer either. It suddenly occurred to me that the whole picture we were presenting to this M.P. was nothing less than bizarre, and that there was not a chance that he was going to send us on our way. The M.P. walked over to a jeep parked on the roadside and talked on the radio for a minute or two. By then traffic was backing up and we were beginning to hear angry shouts. The M.P. returned and told us in no uncertain terms to pull to the side of the road and await further instructions. He touched his sidearm meaningfully and said, "And don't even think about driving away."

We pulled to the side of the road as instructed and waited. A steady stream of military vehicles of all sorts went by, bound in both directions. Trucks full of ammunition, fuel, and other supplies headed east towards the front and empty trucks headed back west to pick up another load. Interspersed among these was an array of combat and combat support vehicles, mostly heading east: Towed and self-propelled artillery pieces, engineer, road building, and bridging equipment, and many strange looking vehicles that neither Moose nor I could identify. I had seen some of our combat units, armored infantry, and artillery in action over the last couple of days, but until now had not realized or even thought about the magnitude of the logistical effort it took to sustain them. It was awesome.

As we sat there waiting, Moose and I took stock. We were now under the control of the U.S. Military and we had a suspicion that they weren't going to know quite how to identify and deal with us. Those first combat units that we'd come in contact with did not question that we were escaped POWs. From the way we appeared and flagged them

130

down and from our tattered condition, they seemed to have no doubts that we were who and what we claimed to be. They had treated us well, but it was clear and understandable that they wanted us gone so that they could get on with fighting the war. But we guessed that now that we were in the rear echelon we would come under much closer scrutiny.

The only identification we had was our POW dog tags. We also guessed that we were among the first POWs to be run into so only a few of our intelligence people would know that these dog tags were authentic. We therefore concluded that we might be suspected of being deserters or even German infiltrators. The M.P., who was still directing traffic and eyeing us, certainly seemed to think we were suspicious characters.

We'd waited and stewed for an hour or so when a jeep pulled up and a captain got out, approached our car and politely introduced himself. He said, "I'm told that you are American pilots escaped from a German prison camp." Moose and I both affirmed that we were. He asked if we had any identification. We showed him our POW dog tags and I started to elaborate, but he held up his hand and said, "I believe you." He indicated the M.P. directing traffic and said, "When the Sergeant called and said he had two scruffy-looking men in ragged clothes driving a big white convertible with a young lady passenger and a couple of cases of booze who said they were escaped POWs headed for Paris, our reaction at the headquarters was that it must be true, 'cause who would make up a story like that." The tension that had been building for the last hour went out and we all laughed.

The Captain said, "I apologize for the delay, but you're the first POWs that our unit has come in contact with and, frankly, we didn't know what to do with you. We called 7th Air Force Headquarters in Paris for guidance and they told us to get you to Paris as soon as possible and they would take over from there."

He told us to follow him back to his headquarters and that we would be taken to a nearby airfield where we would board a DC-3 that was scheduled in that afternoon to deliver an American General and return to Nancy. From there we would go by train to Paris. He said that our passenger would be turned over to the French Liaison for repatriation and that, as far as our "supplies" were concerned, we could take what we could carry and he would "dispose" of the rest. He said he would also find use for our elegant limousine.

We followed the Captain to his headquarters where we said goodbye to Fifi, packed three bottles each in our tattered packs, (we didn't have room for the K-rations) and climbed in a jeep that was to take us to the airfield. As we were about to depart, the Captain came over to the jeep and said, "I am proud to have met you and been able to assist you in your return from hell. I assure you that you will be treated with the dignity and respect that you deserve. God speed!" He stood tall and saluted as the jeep pulled away. Moose and I were deeply moved.

We arrived at the airstrip just as the DC-3 landed and taxied to a stop without shutting down the engines. The General and his aide, the only passengers on board, jumped down and approached our jeep, which was to take him back to the forward U.S. headquarters. Moose and I got out of the jeep and saluted. The General looked at us like we were something that had just crawled out of a hole, but returned our salute without comment and got into the waiting jeep. Moose and I clambered aboard the DC-3. The crew chief gave the pilot thumbs-up, the aircraft roared down the runway, and moments later we were airborne. We flew at about two hundred feet and when I asked the crew chief why, he explained it was to avoid detection – that although the Luftwaffe was almost completely out of business by then, a stray showed up now and then and would attack the lightly armed command and passenger aircraft such as the one we were in. I thought, "Dear God, I've been shot down once in this war, please don't let it happen again." It didn't!

We landed at an airfield in Nancy where we were immediately taken to the train station and put on board an express bound for Paris. There we were picked up by a staff car and, shortly thereafter, with no money, no orders, and dressed in filthy rags, I was standing in the magnificent lobby of the world famous Ritz Hotel in Paris. I wondered if I was going to wake up momentarily and find myself lying on the ground in a tiny hideout in the German forest.

I didn't wake up on the ground; I woke up in a plush bed with the first light of Paris peeking through the window. I lay quietly for a long time reveling in the comfort, my mind cascading through the events of the last nine months: the miracle of surviving the crash, the gut-wrenching fear and uncertainty I experienced in my first days in solitary, the interrogation and accusation of war crimes, surviving from day to day in the Stalags, the horrors on the march to Nuremberg, and, finally, the escape and the last sixteen days that brought me here to the luxury of the finest hotel in the world. I said aloud, "I'm safe now. I beat you bastards and you can't hurt me anymore!" But I knew that I had not been through all of this alone and I thanked God again. I wondered if I could call my mother and my wife to let them know I was safe.

The ringing of the telephone broke my reverie. I picked it up and a soft female voice said, "Lieutenant, this is Corporal Shirley. Major Johnson wants to know if you can make time for breakfast and debriefing?"

I said, "I can certainly make time for breakfast, but that might take the rest of the day." We both laughed and I said, "What time does the Major want me there, and what time is it now? I don't have a watch."

She replied, "It's now seven o'clock. I'll come for you at nine."

I shaved with a new razor blade and took a long bath in real hot water. I then doused my clean body and my tattered clothes with a highly perfumed bathwater, provided by the hotel. This done, I stood at the window looking out over the streets of Paris while I awaited my escort. I wondered how this proud and beautiful city had managed to survive the horrors of the war that had destroyed so much of Europe.

As I followed my escort through the crowded lobby of the hotel I received a lot of stares. I wanted to think it was from the cologne, but suspected it was my overall appearance that attracted so much attention. I felt very much out of place, but had nowhere to hide. Then someone asked, "Are you the escaped POW that I heard about this morning?" When I confirmed that I was, everyone crowded in to shake my hand and congratulate me. I was quite moved and could only nod and murmur, "Thank you" over and over.

Corporal Shirley led me to a table in the dining room where Moose and the Major were already seated drinking coffee. As I approached, it suddenly occurred to me that I didn't know how to address "Moose" in this drastically changed atmosphere. I knew he was a Major, but the only name I knew was Moose. I didn't think "Major Moose" would be appropriate, so I decided just to stick with "Moose" until he told me differently.

I introduced myself to the Major and told Moose that he still looked like a POW but smelled a lot better. We all three laughed at this. The Major indicated the elegantly appointed setting and said, "I expect this beats Nuremberg. Welcome to Paris."

We spent the next hour consuming the most scrumptious meal I had ever eaten. I had to be careful not to eat like a starved pig. I noticed that Moose seemed to be struggling for restraint too. We mainly nodded and grunted as the Major brought us up to date on the situation in Europe and as much as he knew about the war in the Pacific. We were shocked and saddened to hear of the death of President Roosevelt. The Major told us that the whole nation and the free world were in mourning.

When we had finished breakfast the Major said that arrangements had been made to get us proper clothing, uniforms and civvies, and a portion of our back pay that was due. He then told us that we could be shipped home as early as the next day or, if we wanted, we could take a couple of weeks R and R in the Mediterranean. I immediately opted for home. Moose surprised me by saying that he'd like to think about it.

I spent the rest of the day alternately being debriefed and preparing for transfer to Camp Lucky Strike, the embarkation point for all G.I.s headed home. That evening, Moose and I went to a small restaurant near the hotel that had been recommended by Corporal Shirley. We were invited to join a group of officers who asked us a lot of questions about our captivity and escape. We were both tired and excused ourselves early to return to the hotel. On the way up in the elevator, Moose turned to me and said, "I guess this is goodbye. I've decided to take some R and R and spend some time winding down before I go home."

I was suddenly overcome and for several moments could not speak. I had the greatest respect and admiration for this big man but realized I knew so little about him. During the eighteen days we'd spent sharing the danger and intense emotions, we had never discussed our personal lives. Our shared goal had been survival and it was only on that level that we had communicated. I didn't even know his real name or if he was married and had a family. When we got off the elevator Moose put his arms around me and said, "Take care, my friend." As he walked off towards his room, I found enough voice to reply, "Go with God, Moose."

EPILOGUE

Camp Lucky Strike was a huge facility set up by the military to process and ship American soldiers home. In the months following V.E. Day, several million soldiers, including ex-POWs, would pass through its gates. The physical and mental condition of these men and women varied widely, but their spirits were universally high - they were going home!

When I arrived at Camp Lucky Strike, I was not a pretty sight. I had lost forty pounds over the period of captivity and the clothes that I'd been given in Paris were not tailored for skin and bones. My whole body, including the visible parts, was covered with bites from fleas and a myriad of other critters that infested the prison camps and the woods where we'd taken refuge along the way. My cheekbones stuck out and my eyes were so deep in their sockets that I barely had peripheral vision. To add to all of this, I had gingivitis so bad that several doctors who examined me told me that my teeth would fall out in the not too distant future.

I spent three days at Lucky Strike and was then moved to London where I was put on a troop ship in a convoy headed for home. German U-Boats were still running loose in the Atlantic so cruisers and destroyers escorted us. Fortunately, the passage was made without incident.

I was assigned a bunk in a cabin with forty other G.I.s. While going through my meager belongings I discovered that I still had one bottle of Hennessy left. I knew that it wouldn't be safe under prevailing living conditions and I'd had enough brandy in Paris so, after careful consideration, I decided to put it to work for me. I gave it to the head cook. It paid off handsomely. I don't want to indicate the cook could be influenced, but I think it helped. He sat with me while I ate and asked many questions about the war. For the next twelve nights, I was invited to the kitchen for a "midnight snack," consisting of fresh baked bread, butter, strawberry jam, and a couple of glasses of milk. I was also allowed to attend both settings for each of the three regular meals. I ate like a starved animal, which of course I was. It seemed like I spent the entire trip eating or lying on my bunk thinking about eating. By the time we docked in New Jersey, I'd gained ten pounds and had conquered the hunger that had been part of my life for the past nine months, but never again would be.

From New Jersey, I went by train to San Francisco, where I was immediately put on sixty days' leave and told that I would be notified where to report when my leave was over. From there I went by train to Los Angeles where my wife, Barbara, whom I hardly knew, and my mother met me. They were both appalled by my skeletal, flea-bitten appearance, but I assured them that I was on the mend and that they should have seen me a month ago.

Barbara, who was the assistant manager and receptionist at Elizabeth Arden's "Red Door Beauty Salon," the "Beauty Salon of the Stars," located on Sunset Strip, had a plan. She arranged for me to get the "Super Star" treatment at the salon. Every other day for the next two months I got a steam bath, a body massage, a scalp massage, and a facial, and all as the guest of Elizabeth Arden. With that, a strict regimen of exercise, and a lot of Southern California sunshine, I began to look and feel like a healthy young fighter pilot.

One night during this period, the manager of the Elizabeth Arden Salon invited Barbara and me to a Saturday night dinner at her home. There were some twenty other guests there, most of them from the motion picture industry. I was sitting on a couch enjoying a drink while Barbara moved freely, chatting with the other guests, most of whom she knew from the salon. The salon manager's husband, Manny Wolfe, a distinguished looking gentleman, came over and joined me. He said that his wife told him that I had been a POW and was now the salon's favorite client. I laughed and said that they were using me as a "Before and After" to prove just how good they were. He asked me several questions about my experiences as a fighter pilot and as a prisoner of war. He asked me what I planned to do after the war. I told him that I planned to spend all the money that had accrued while I was a POW and then I didn't know what I was going to do. We both laughed at this and I guessed that he probably knew, as I did, that my "nest egg" wouldn't amount to as much as the cost of this dinner party and wouldn't last very long.

He turned serious and said, "I have great respect and admiration for you and all like you who have sacrificed so much while life went on for the rest of us." He handed me his business card and added, "Please come and see me when you're out of the service. I may be able to help you find a vocation you enjoy."

It was about the middle of July when my leave time was over and I was ordered to report to the Del Mar Beach Club. This turned out to be a beautiful hotel and social club located, as the name would imply, right on the beach in Santa Monica, California. It had been taken over by the Air Force and was being used as a facility to debrief and evaluate the physical and mental health of ex-POWs and other servicemen returning from combat duty in Europe. I assumed that all of us there were being considered for service in the Pacific Theatre. Wives were invited, and Barbara and I were put up in a luxurious room overlooking the beach where, between a myriad of physical and mental tests, we spent a lot of time in the sand, surf and sunshine. It was like a second honeymoon.

About the 10th day, I was called in and asked if I would be willing to go to the Pacific - that they needed fighter pilots there. I was not only willing, but I wanted to do this. I had plenty of points to get out of the service but I still wanted to verify my skills and help my country. I said, "Yes." I was given orders to report to Luke Air Force Base in Phoenix for refresher training in preparation for duty in the Pacific.

Apparently I had passed muster, because I reported in at Luke about the first of August and had just begun the refresher training when, on August 6th, 1945, a U.S. Air Force bomber took off from a tiny Pacific Island and flew into history. This event, and the one that followed three days later, would not only end the war; it changed life on our planet as we knew it.

The end of the war brought the end to what I will always consider the most exciting and turbulent chapter in my life. On December 4, 1945, I walked out of Luke Air Force Base in civilian clothes with my head held high and great hope for the future.

EPILOGUE II

I sat in my private office overlooking Sunset Strip reflecting on my good fortune. I had been discharged from the service in December of 1945. By January of 1946, my savings had shrunk to a level which required refurbishing. Remembering the card I had received from Manny Wolfe at the dinner party, I dug it out and found that I would be talking to the Executive Producer at RKO Studios. It was one of my more brilliant decisions because in 3 weeks I was hired by Marx, Miller & Marx, a boutique motion picture agency in Hollywood. Barbara Stanwyck, Ray Milland, Fred McMurray, and Glenn Ford were just a few of the top stars they represented. I knew no more about being an agent than I had known about being a carpenter, but in short order, Gummo Marx took me under his wing and I found myself spending most of my time visiting radio agencies and lunching at the Brown Derby. Life was good. War was forgotten, or maybe memory was put on hold.

As I was pondering these things, I was startled by a knock on the door. I said, "Yes?" and was even more startled when Harpo Marx opened the door and said, "Are you busy? May I come in?"

I said, "Of course, Mr. Marx."

He put me at ease with his famous grin and said, "Please, call me Harpo."

I managed "Yes sir, Mr. Marx," as he sat down in the big leather chair facing my desk.

I had been told by several people that Harpo was not really a mute, but it was always said with a wink and a grin, so I wasn't sure, until now.

Harpo had just seated himself when there was another knock on the door and Groucho stuck his head in. When he saw Harpo, he said, "Well,

139

I see you have enough Marxes for today. I'll talk to you later." Before I could find voice, he shut the door and was gone.

Harpo sat and visited for about thirty minutes, mostly asking about my background and particularly my time as a POW. He was quite easy to talk to and seemed genuinely interested in what I had to say.

While we were chatting, the phone rang and Vivian, Gummo Marx's secretary, said that there was going to be a meeting in the conference room and would I please inform Harpo. She added that I was invited also.

I followed Harpo into the meeting where he introduced me to Groucho, Zeppo, and Chico. I had already met, and in fact been interviewed by Gummo Marx and Alan Miller, who were also present.

I sat in awe for the next hour or more as each of the Marx Brothers told what he had been engaged in for the last several weeks. There was a lot of joking and laughter much like they did on screen. I couldn't wait to get home and tell Barbara and my mother all about my day.

I stayed with the agency for two years until I felt comfortable with life again and decided it was time to finish my interrupted education and move on. It had been a great period of learning and growth for me and I've been forever grateful to Alan Miller and the Marx Brothers for taking me in and helping me through this transition period. When I said goodbye, Groucho and Harpo both told me that I should write about my experiences as a pilot and a prisoner of war. So here, some sixty years later, I'm doing just that. I sincerely hope they approve of what I have said.

ISBN 1412068874-6

9 781412 068741